D1550703

"Andy Cook is an amazing pastor/teacher who is passionate for Jerusalem. He loves to talk and teach about Jewish history, bringing the Old and New Testaments together for the complete Word of God!"

—ROBERT D'ANDREA, president,
Christian Television Network

"I have traveled the ancient paths of Israel many times, and know the priceless value of walking through the land of the Bible. Don't miss the lessons these paths have for us. Treasure this book. You're not only going to be delighted . . . you're going to be changed!"

—DR. JOHNNY HUNT, pastor,
Woodstock First Baptist Church and former president,
Southern Baptist Convention

SECRETS *from* ANCIENT PATHS

ANDY COOK

Kregel
Publications

This book is dedicated to the memory of

my mother-in-law, Melrose Evans.

This is what the LORD says:

"Stand at the crossroads and look;
  ask for the ancient paths,
ask where the good way is, and walk in it,
  and you will find rest for your souls."

JEREMIAH 6:16

ACKNOWLEDGMENTS

MANY YEARS AGO, a professor at my seminary unfolded the Bible like no one had ever done for me before. Dr. Richard Spencer took the land of Israel, the academics of New Testament study, and the familiar stories of Jesus and the early church, and produced lectures that held us spellbound. There were mysteries being solved in that class, and we couldn't get enough.

On one occasion, he mistakenly scheduled a final exam one class-day early, which meant our semester ended before time was officially up. Under normal conditions, such a day would be treated as a surprise holiday. In seminary, we might have even called it a gift from God! But this class was different. Out of a hope that he might show up anyway, I went to our classroom at our scheduled class time.

The room was packed. All of us wanted to know the secrets from the ancient paths. And, much to our delight, Dr. Spencer came and gave us another hour of insight. What this man was sharing was so intriguing, it didn't really matter if the grades were set and the course was completed. If there was a chance he might teach again, we'd be there. In three years, I sat under his teaching as often as possible. He was the first to show me that there was much to learn from the land of the Bible, and he created in me a passion to walk the ancient paths myself.

Since that time, I've met many other great teachers, but none better than Ray Vander Laan. Visit Israel, and you'll tour many ruins. Visit Israel with Ray, and he'll make the rocks talk. My 2009 trip to Israel with him turned out to be a life-changing experience. Someone once asked me, "What exactly changed?" Part of me wanted to ask, "What *didn't* change?" But instead I replied, "The passion. He showed me what passion for following Jesus looked like."

And I wanted that passion. We live in an age when information is available everywhere. Passion, however, is a rare commodity. Passion for following our rabbi is even rarer. I am a better follower of Jesus because I've had the chance to walk with Ray Vander Laan.

For all my teachers, and for the volumes of books and resources they have directed my way, I am thankful. My words in this book are, in part, little more than a mixture of their words.

I am also grateful to Israel's Ministry of Tourism and the Christian Television Network for their partnership in allowing me to teach on location at so many biblical sites. God has allowed us to do a great work together, and I am humbled.

I owe a great debt to the people of Shirley Hills Baptist Church in Warner Robins, Georgia. They have supported my dreams, my travels, my writing, and my family far more than I could have ever expected.

I am also grateful to the Board of Directors at Experience Israel Now, Inc. What an honor to work with such a talented group!

And closest to my heart is my family. Our family tree is grounded in a long history of men and women who followed Jesus with an "all-in" attitude. My parents handed that legacy to me, one patient day at a time.

My wife, Melody, is the only woman I've ever loved, and I would not be following my dream if she hadn't followed me. Over the past thirty-plus years, we've grown up with three incredible girls—Summer, Melinda, and Courtney—and thrown one wedding (glad to finally have another guy around,

Mike!). Now we're grandparents, and yes, there are photos. Life is good, for we're all on the journey together.

Finally, I am thankful for *you*. If you've chosen this book, you're after the same passion I'm after. In a sense, you're standing at the crossroads, asking for the right way. Thank you for asking. You've made me a better traveler, for nothing energizes me more than telling the story to those who want to hear it.

Let's take the good way together.

Rest for our souls is waiting.

HIDDEN IN
PLAIN SIGHT

A FRIEND OF MINE once served in a covert corner of the American military forces. He was part of the "Special Ops" (or Special Operations) that trained for and carried out secret missions around the world.

This was clandestine work. Secret stuff. They always faced great danger as they worked. As a result, they worked very hard not to be discovered.

"We had a problem," he once told me. "How do you hide a huge airplane filled with Special Ops forces and all their equipment?"

The answer? You hide them in plain sight. If you need to hide an airplane, hide it among other airplanes . . . at an airport. If you need to hide highly trained troops, make them look like the other people at an airport. If there are already hundreds of passengers, airport workers, and delivery personnel swarming over the property, simply blend in as passengers, airport workers, or delivery workers.

Did it work? "Every time," my friend laughed. "We were in, we were out, and they never knew we were there."

The Bible has a few secrets, too. Hidden among all the words, and all the stories, are a handful of details that can transform even the most familiar passages of Scripture. In a sense, the information that is there wasn't hidden at all. The details are very much in plain sight. And yet most people miss them. Since most of us don't live in the land of the Bible, we miss the insight the land can give us. Since most Christians aren't Jewish, we miss the impact of our incredible Jewish heritage. And frankly, since most of us aren't as committed students of the text as the first followers of Jesus were, we miss much of what is "hidden" from us, even though the words are right before our eyes. The full impact of the Bible's words might as well be on a covert mission, slipping into our times of Bible study, and slipping out, unnoticed and undiscovered.

It's time to discover those secrets.

Take the day when Jesus said this:

> *Come to me, all you who are weary and burdened, and I will give you rest. Take my yoke upon you and learn from me, for I am gentle and humble in heart, and you will find rest for your souls.* (Matthew 11:28–29)

Familiar words? Of course! Most followers of Christ would recognize the words as some of the most comforting you'd ever want to hear. But there is also something else here. There is more here than meets the eye. And those who heard Jesus speak the words in person knew the secret.

In that case, they knew Jesus was quoting one of the prophets. Like Jesus, most of the people in his audience that day had already memorized Jeremiah's words.

> *This is what the Lord says:*
>
> *"Stand at the crossroads and look;*
> *ask for the ancient paths,*
> *ask where the good way is, and walk in it,*
> *and you will find rest for your souls. (Jeremiah 6:16)*

"... *rest for your souls.*" Jeremiah had held it out like a tantalizing offer. It's as if he had said, "If you'll look for it, you can have it. If you'll ask for it, it will be given to you! So when you come to the crossroads—when you come to a place of decision making—stop and ask for help. The right path is there. It's been there all along. It's an *ancient* path. Walk here, and you shall find rest for the deepest part of you. Rest for your souls."

Note that Jeremiah said these words weren't his words. This message was from God. I like to picture a wild-eyed prophet making sure his audience got the point. "THIS . . . is what the LORD says!"

Unfortunately, many in Jeremiah's generation missed the point. They missed the ancient path. Jeremiah's generation found tragedy and hardship, and much of it had come from their own poor choices. Like us, they had moments that served as "crossroads." All too often, they rushed forward without asking for guidance. They made far too many choices without regard to God's instructions. They ignored the words that could have saved them heartache, destruction, and exile.

As a result, they missed the rest for the soul that could have come from following the ancient paths. The words were in plain view for them, as well as us. But because they didn't consider them, the words remained "hidden." The good way, the good path, was empty.

Jesus began his ministry with a simple invitation for those who would be his disciples. "Walk with me," he said. "Follow me." There were many trying to decide if they should follow. To those who would listen, he said,

> *Come to me, all you who are weary and burdened, and I will give you rest. Take my yoke upon you and learn from me, for I am gentle and humble in heart, and you will find rest for your souls. (Matthew 11:28–29)*

Some were old enough to have become jaded to religious offers of peace. Some were worn down by the difficulty of keeping all the rules God required of them. Some were just tired. Fatigued. Ready to quit.

"Come with me," Jesus seemed to be saying. "I'll show you the way. Remember what Jeremiah offered? I'll show you the ancient path. I'll show you the good way. I'll give you rest for your souls. I'll give you what you've always wanted. I'll satisfy that longing that has long existed in the deepest part of who you are. I'll give you rest . . . *rest for your soul*."

It was an echo of what Jeremiah had said were God's words from long ago. Too many people had missed the right path for far too long. So Jesus came, and he had said he'd come to show the way. Actually, Jesus said he *was* the way. "I *am* the way," he said in John 14:6. In the language of the New Testament, "way" is also "path."

I am the path . . .

From time to time, all of us stand at the crossroads. Every day, we have choices to make. Consequences will follow those choices as surely as gravity causes apples to fall from trees. Make the right choice, and we'll enjoy the consequences. Make the wrong choice, and we'll regret the consequences.

So ask where the good way is. Listen to the offer again.

"Come to me," Jesus said, "and you will find rest for your souls."

Jesus is the right path. The right way. So follow Jesus. Pause at the crossroads every day. Ask him for the right way, the good way . . . the ancient way. If you walk in that way, you'll find the best life you've ever known. It will have trouble, hardship, joy, and celebration. And yet there will be purpose all along the way, and a quiet confidence that you've found the right way.

Call it a deep satisfaction. Call it a peace that passes all understanding. Or if you like, use an ancient phrase. Call it "rest for your soul."

So, are there really "secrets" to be found along the ancient paths? Sure there are. However, once you find them, you'll see that these "secrets" were "hidden" in plain sight. In a sense, the dust of time and culture has covered them up. What we'll seek to do is travel back in time to the original setting. We will need to remove the lens of our culture and look through the lens of the Bible's cultures. Difficult? Perhaps, at first. Possible? Very much so.

There are secrets begging to be discovered.

So let's get started.

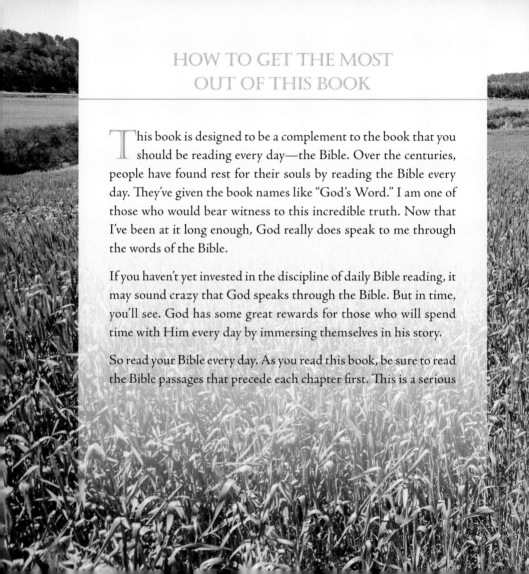

HOW TO GET THE MOST
OUT OF THIS BOOK

This book is designed to be a complement to the book that you should be reading every day—the Bible. Over the centuries, people have found rest for their souls by reading the Bible every day. They've given the book names like "God's Word." I am one of those who would bear witness to this incredible truth. Now that I've been at it long enough, God really does speak to me through the words of the Bible.

If you haven't yet invested in the discipline of daily Bible reading, it may sound crazy that God speaks through the Bible. But in time, you'll see. God has some great rewards for those who will spend time with Him every day by immersing themselves in his story.

So read your Bible every day. As you read this book, be sure to read the Bible passages that precede each chapter first. This is a serious request. You'll maximize what God wants to do with the words of this book if you'll first read the words of his book. You might even want to use your Bible to read more than simply the words printed here. Knowing the entire context of the passage is often key to understanding the passage. So don't hesitate to read more than what's printed inside these pages!

At the end of each chapter in this book, you'll find a short section of application called "Make the Lesson Your Own." Don't skip over this. It's extremely important. Knowledge without application is useless. Do your best to connect the line from the Bible's message to your own life, and then follow the Bible's instructions.

The result? Rest for your soul.

—Andy Cook
January 2013

⌒ MATTHEW 25:1–13 ⌒

At that time the kingdom of heaven will be like ten virgins who took their lamps and went out to meet the bridegroom. Five of them were foolish and five were wise. The foolish ones took their lamps but did not take any oil with them. The wise, however, took oil in jars along with their lamps. The bridegroom was a long time in coming, and they all became drowsy and fell asleep.

At midnight the cry rang out: "Here's the bridegroom! Come out to meet him!"

Then all the virgins woke up and trimmed their lamps. The foolish ones said to the wise, "Give us some of your oil; our lamps are going out."

"No," they replied, "there may not be enough for both us and you. Instead, go to those who sell oil and buy some for yourselves."

But while they were on their way to buy the oil, the bridegroom arrived. The virgins who were ready went in with him to the wedding banquet. And the door was shut.

Later the others also came. "Sir! Sir!" they said. "Open the door for us!"

But he replied, "I tell you the truth, I don't know you."

Therefore keep watch, because you do not know the day or the hour.

THE PARABLE OF
THE SELFISH VIRGINS

TEN VIRGINS, JESUS SAID, wanted to go to a wedding.

Have you ever paid attention to young girls at a wedding? For many of them, it's a fantasy come true. It's the dress-up party of the year, and the bride looks like Cinderella. There's a party and dancing and music and flowers and a dreamy groom . . .

To a young girl, it's a setting right out of the movies.

This isn't to say guys don't like a good wedding, too. After all, there's good food, good friends . . . and Cinderella to boot. Let's face it. A wedding can be the best party you'll ever attend.

The ten girls in Jesus' parable had no intention of missing the party. Maybe the girls were right on the edge of their teen years. Just breaking into the world of grown-up love stories, just starting to understand the pull of one heart toward another. They *really, really* wanted to be a part of the wedding celebration.

But the wedding was late. With the night came darkness. Five of the girls had oil for their lamps, Jesus said, and five did not. Short end of the story? The wedding started, people joined the procession, but only those with working lamps were admitted to the evening of the year.

When this became obvious, the five girls without oil—the "unwise" virgins—begged the girls who had oil for a little fuel. If they had been around today, they would have been begging for fresh batteries for their flashlights. But in that day, it was oil for their lamps. The girls with oil said no, and told their desperate friends to go buy some. At that hour, that was an impossible task, and once the wedding was ready to start, someone shut the door. The way Jesus tells the story, there's no doubt the door won't be opened again, no matter what. It was a one-time opportunity, and only the five virgins with working lamps got to see Cinderella and her prince. So goes the parable of the selfish virgins.

Actually, there is no parable of the selfish virgins. It's just one of the uncomfortable thoughts that sticks in the back of your mind as you read of Jesus telling one of his famous stories.

The selfishness has never bothered you? Surely you've heard the story and wondered why Jesus didn't just make an application about sharing. Is this the best way to live out the "Golden Rule" Jesus gave in his Sermon on the Mount? If this is the way to live out a "Do unto others as you would have them do unto you" lifestyle, we're in for a rough life! Sharing is an admirable principle.

More than that, sharing is commanded. Prophets like Isaiah (Isaiah 58:7) and Ezekiel (Ezekiel 18) put sharing squarely in the middle of what it means to be a righteous person. In their debate with Job, Job's friends openly questioned whether or not Job had shared his possessions with others (Job 22).

No doubt about it. Sharing with others is a core value of what it means to be righteous. The concept fits in practically any sermon.

But not this time.

The reason no one listening to Jesus cried out a judgment against the five "selfish" virgins is that they knew the girls weren't selfish at all. Let's look at the parable from the perspective of the original audience.

If you've ever lived away from the city lights, perhaps you'll understand the story better than others. It can get plenty dark at night when there are no streetlights. If you go outside at night, a good flashlight might just save your life.

There might be a snake on the ground. Poisonous or not, if you step on a snake in the dark, you'll face an instant stress test and wish to God you'd carried a light. Or there might be nothing more than a hole in the ground that could lead to a sprained ankle. You might hear a rustling in the bushes and wonder whether you're about to be attacked by a ferocious beast. So what if it was only a house cat? The darkness is frightening!

When the Bible speaks of itself, it says that it is a lamp to our feet (Psalm 119:105). This is the idea. There are times when just a little bit of illumination can make all the difference. It can save us time, save us stress, and even save our life.

So we carry flashlights and make sure the batteries are good. If you're an experienced outdoorsperson, you'll carry some extra batteries with you. You'll change them before you're left in the dark. You'll have a stash of extras on a shelf at home. A flashlight needs batteries the way an oil lamp needs oil.

The word we have for people without extra batteries? Let's just say there's a lot of regret if your flashlight runs low and you've imagined a snake or two stretched out somewhere on the path ahead!

The word we have for a person who has plenty of batteries on hand is "wise." Everyone knows flashlight batteries will eventually wear out, so a wise person will have extras on hand.

The kind of oil lamp Jesus and his audience would have known can be held in the palm of one hand. The oil jug that was its partner was just as small. It didn't take a lot of oil to keep a lamp burning, and like all fuel, oil wasn't cheap. People didn't carry a lot of it. Parents didn't let their daughters take enough to share with their friends. There may have been no more oil in an oil jug than just enough to refill a lamp one time.

But as it turns out, a single refill was just enough to get into the wedding.

There were a lot of unknowns about weddings in Jesus' day. No one knew exactly when the wedding would be, for instance. You'd have some hints, but only when the bridegroom's father told his son that the house he'd built for the new couple was ready could the groom go for his bride. The moment the father gave the go-ahead, the groom took off. He rallied his friends and they started a parade that wound through the village until they arrived at the bride's home. The groom would be joined by his bride and the parade continued through the village to the location of the wedding, picking up other guests as it wound through the village. The wedding would eventually follow, and the party would last for hours.

Rules were rules, and young girls simply weren't allowed out into the night without their lamps, and without enough oil to keep their path well lit. For five girls left in an empty, dark village? It must have been a very sad, very frightening experience.

Five girls were well-prepared and made it to the party. Five were looking for oil when they were locked out. It's a really sad ending for five girls who, in effect, didn't have extra batteries for their flashlights.

Five girls were wise. They weren't

selfish. They had only enough oil for themselves, and no more. It wasn't their responsibility to supply their friends with oil. They had prepared for the wedding well, and it was their right to enjoy the party.

The key to understanding this story is the context of the conversation. Jesus wasn't trying to get as many people as he could into a wedding. He was trying to convince people they needed to be ready for judgment! He had just warned his listeners that a day of reckoning would come "as it was in the days of Noah" (Matthew 24:37). It would, therefore, be a day with no recourse for those who weren't prepared. And by the end of his trio of parables in Matthew 25, there was no doubt that some would be so unprepared for judgment that there would be "weeping and gnashing of teeth" (Matthew 25:30) and a departure into "eternal punishment" (Matthew 25:46).

With hell as an option, the idea of missing the party is frightening. Terrifying even. But listen to the positive spin of what Jesus was saying: Don't go into eternity terrified of hell. Instead, do whatever it takes to be ready for the celebration of heaven! Live in such a way that it's obvious you've connected with what it means to follow Jesus. Use your God-given skills for God's glory, like the wise servants who invested their master's money. That's the lesson of the parable that follows the story of the ten young girls. And as the third parable of the Matthew 25 trilogy illustrates, this life will so naturally result in sharing food with the hungry, housing with the homeless, and comfort for the sick, you could separate the righteous from the unrighteous the way a shepherd separates the sheep from the goats.

So listen to Jesus as he urges us to be ready for eternity.

Like a girl getting ready for a wedding, you've got to be prepared.

In a very real sense, making sure you get into the best celebration any of us could ever imagine is a decision. You've got to think ahead and be ready.

But it's not oil for a lamp that we need.

It's Jesus that we need.

Deciding to follow Jesus is a decision you and you alone can make. This is the lesson of the parable. No one can make this most important of all decisions for you. In the story Jesus told, there was only enough oil for each girl wise enough to be prepared for the celebration. In this life? There's only enough decision-making ability in you for one person. Your mother? She has only enough for her. Your dad? Same thing. Your favorite pastor? He might deliver a lot of invitations, but when it comes to heaven, he can only make the decision to go for himself. He can't decide for any of his listeners, no matter how much he might want all of them to know the joy of eternal security.

The wedding's coming. The invitations are out. Are you going?

Jesus spent much of his teaching time urging people to be ready for eternity.

The story of the ten virgins is followed by a troubling story of a returning master who wants an account of how his servants had—or hadn't—invested his resources. The final story deals with separating a mixed flock of sheep and goats in the final judgment.

You don't want to be a goat.

The decision to follow Jesus involves a few simple steps. It may seem relatively easy to take the initial plunge of belief. However, living the faith for the rest of your life will be the biggest challenge you've ever known. So it's no minor decision.

Nevertheless, these are the steps:

1. Know that God loves you.

   For God so loved the world that he gave his one and only Son, that whoever believes in him shall not perish but have eternal life. (John 3:16)

2. Admit your sin to God.

   For all have sinned and fall short of the glory of God. (Romans 3:23)

3. Believe that Jesus is God's son and that he died on the cross for our sins.

   While we were still sinners, Christ died for us. (Romans 5:8)

4. Tell others that you've decided to follow Jesus.

   If you declare with your mouth, "Jesus is Lord," and believe in your heart that God raised him from the dead, you will be saved. (Romans 10:9)

The parable of the ten young girls is about a wedding. So give a wedding some thought. Sooner or later, in every wedding someone asks, "Do you want this person as your mate for life?" And no matter how shy the bride, no matter how badly the groom stutters, all who have heard the question wait for the answer. They wait for an audible, clearly understood "Yes" or "No."

There's no real plan b for a "No." There won't be a marriage with a "No." There's no reception for a "No." There's no honeymoon, no family, no anniversaries with a "No."

But with a "Yes," everything changes. Two become one. A party breaks out, signaling the beginning of a great adventure. As time goes by in that great adventure, children may enter into the picture. The stories that will be retold for decades are collected year by year.

That's what a "Yes" does at a wedding.

So Jesus has laid out the invitation. He's the groom, and we're the bride. He's asked the question, and he waits for an answer. From you, from me, from everyone. Remember the lesson of the oil jug: No one else can answer for you. We each have to make the decision for ourselves.

Say "Yes."

It changes everything.

↜ PSALM 24:3−4 ↝

Who may ascend the hill of the LORD?
    Who may stand in his holy place?
He who has clean hands and a pure heart,
    who does not lift up his soul to an idol
    or swear by what is false.

↜ JOHN 2:6−8 ↝

Nearby stood six stone water jars, the kind used by the Jews for ceremonial washing, each holding from twenty to thirty gallons.

    Jesus said to the servants, "Fill the jars with water"; so they filled them to the brim.

    Then he told them, "Now draw some out and take it to the master of the banquet."

CLEAN HANDS . . .
AND A PURE HEART

I T MIGHT BE the most famous miracle in world history.

That's so ironic. It really wasn't even all that important. This miracle dealt with nothing more than providing refreshments at a party! Still, it would be hard to find a person who hasn't heard that Jesus once turned water into wine.

But there is more to this miracle than first meets the wine glass. John, the young disciple who recorded the story for us, calls it a "sign." This miracle, apparently, is supposed to tell us something. Like a sign on the road, it'll give us key information. Direction. Help. As it was for the guests at that wedding, it might even refresh us!

You know the story, I'm sure. Jesus and his disciples, plus his mother and a host of friends from the community, were invited to a wedding in Cana. The unnamed couple enjoying the wedding party had no idea that they'd run out of wine, but the mother of Jesus knew, and she knew Jesus could do something about it.

Indeed, he could. And he did. The wedding was saved, the wine flowed, and the servants who knew they'd drawn nothing but water from a place of hand-washing were stunned.

Flabbergasted. Speechless. Nothing short of a miracle!

The servants knew only water had been poured into the six water pots, which were "the kind used by the Jews for ceremonial washing, each holding from twenty to thirty gallons" (John 2:6).

When it comes to props, the stone water pots are the stars of this story. They held somewhere between 120 and 180 gallons of water.

My first observation? That's going to be a *lot* of wine! My second observation? Why was there so much ceremonial water at a wedding?

Water has always been an important part of expressing faith in the Judeo-Christian heritage. Christians are familiar with baptism, the outward sign of an internal decision to follow Jesus. Jewish people know about ceremonial washing, too. In fact, they were using water for ceremonial purposes long before Jesus arrived. Remember John the Baptist? He didn't have to explain to anyone in his Jewish audience why he wanted them to get in the water, or what would happen once they entered the Jordan River. Before Jesus recruited his first disciple, John the Baptist's listeners seemed to know what baptism was, and even how to go about it.

There are other evidences that ceremonial washing by the Jewish people was very common. Pilate famously communicated his innocence over the death of Jesus by washing his hands. It was a symbol the crowd would have instantly understood.

Or what of the day of Pentecost when three thousand people were baptized?

Ever wondered where this mass immersion took place? As it turns out, archeologists have found several first-century *micvahs* all around the southwestern corner of the Temple Mount. A *micvah* was a place of ceremonial immersion. It had steps, it had lots of water, and looked suspiciously like a baptistery used by many Christian churches today. *Micvahs* provide more evidence that water was already being used as a religious symbol long before Christian baptism was practiced.

With that in mind, consider the words of Psalm 24.

> *The earth is the LORD's, and everything in it,*
> *the world, and all who live in it;*
> *for he founded it upon the seas*
> *and established it upon the waters.*

> *Who may ascend the hill of the LORD?*
> *Who may stand in his holy place? (Psalm 24:1–3)*

This psalm is a great one to read or quote in an outdoor setting. Remember being awed by the grandeur of the mountains, the oceans, the stars of a night sky, or a waterfall cascading down a great cliff? What a Creator!

All that God created seems to be so perfect.

All that we are seems to be so imperfect. Ever asked the question of Psalm 24? Who, knowing all that is wrong with us, can possibly approach a God so creative, so powerful, and so holy? Here's the answer: the one "who has clean hands and a pure heart" (Psalm 24:4).

As people considered the message, they wanted to act it out. As they came to places like the Temple, they washed before going to the place of worship. Visit the ruins of ancient synagogues in Israel, and you'll almost certainly find a *micvah* there, too. Archeologists have even uncovered *micvahs* in some of the wealthier homes of the day.

In Jerusalem, at the Temple, one *micvah* would never suffice for the great crowds. That's why there were so many places of ceremonial washing around the Temple Mount. Before people would go up to the Temple ("the hill of the LORD"), they wanted to be right with God. So they slipped into the water, cleansing themselves of all the dirt and grime they would have picked up on the way to Jerusalem. But while they washed, they also asked God for forgiveness. They wanted to be clean not only on the outside, but also on the inside. In fact, washing in a *micvah* was a lot more about internal purity than outer cleanliness.

When Jesus was alive, this tradition of ceremonial washing was one of the most familiar of all the Jewish traditions. And in Cana, it surfaced right at the entrance to a wedding. A wedding—for all the celebration that it is—is also a sacred experience. It is a worship service. Before the people of Cana would

come before God, they would have taken a reflective moment to wash their hands. They wanted clean hands . . . and pure hearts.

The pure heart is obviously much more important than clean hands. Nevertheless, the washing is important, too. And Jesus would take this very symbolic water, turn it into wine—which would later become symbolic of his blood—and save the day for a nameless couple who didn't even know they had a catering problem.

It's also interesting that there were six of the stone jars. Seven has a tradition of being the "perfect" number. So six is one short of "perfection." Perhaps John was telling us, by including this detail, that Perfection had just walked through the door! Without Jesus, the wedding was in trouble. With Jesus, the day was saved.

And what a lot of water! Talk about overkill. Only a small amount of water was needed for the biggest of weddings Cana would ever see. But this wedding feast had perhaps 150 gallons of water on hand in stone containers that would be allowed for ceremonial use over and over and over again. This was enough water to cleanse the world, for all time to come!

It was all wonderfully symbolic. All designed to point us to our own sinfulness, and to the grace of God that was now living among God's people in the person of Jesus. In time, these people would know him as a great miracle worker, and they would look back on this day, remembering the very first amazing thing that Jesus had done. More importantly, some of them would also realize, in time, that what he had done was symbolic of the forgiveness he offered.

Forgiveness that is still available, right now.

MAKE THE LESSON YOUR OWN

Want to do something special? Have a time of prayer, asking God to forgive your sins. Thank Jesus again for dying for your sins. But before you pray? Wash your hands. No kidding. Do this. Put the Scripture into practice. No one has to know . . . just wash your hands, and then pray to be right before your God. You'll be amazed at the difference it makes to *feel* forgiveness.

If you're up for a bigger challenge, memorize the words of Psalm 24 this week. You may never look at water in the same way!

Clean hands. A pure heart. Refreshed by God's grace.

⮜ LUKE 15:11–32 ⮞

Jesus continued: "There was a man who had two sons. The younger one said to his father, 'Father, give me my share of the estate.' So he divided his property between them.

"Not long after that, the younger son got together all he had, set off for a distant country and there squandered his wealth in wild living. After he had spent everything, there was a severe famine in that whole country, and he began to be in need. So he went and hired himself out to a citizen of that country, who sent him to his fields to feed pigs. He longed to fill his stomach with the pods that the pigs were eating, but no one gave him anything.

"When he came to his senses, he said, 'How many of my father's hired servants have food to spare, and here I am starving to death! I will set out and go back to my father and say to him: Father, I have sinned against heaven and against you. I am no longer worthy to be called your son; make me like one of your hired men.' So he got up and went to his father.

"But while he was still a long way off, his father saw him and was filled with compassion for him; he ran to his son, threw his arms around him and kissed him.

"The son said to him, 'Father, I have sinned against heaven and against you. I am no longer worthy to be called your son.'

"But the father said to his servants, 'Quick! Bring the best robe and put it on him. Put a ring on his finger and sandals on his feet. Bring the fattened calf and kill it. Let's have a feast and celebrate. For this son of mine was dead and is alive again; he was lost and is found.' So they began to celebrate.

"Meanwhile, the older son was in the field. When he came near the house, he heard music and dancing. So he called one of the servants and asked him what was going on. 'Your brother has come,' he replied, 'and your father has killed the fattened calf because he has him back safe and sound.'

"The older brother became angry and refused to go in. So his father went out and pleaded with him. But he answered his father, 'Look! All these years I've been slaving for you and never disobeyed your orders. Yet you never gave me even a young goat so I could celebrate with my friends. But when this son of yours who has squandered your property with prostitutes comes home, you kill the fattened calf for him!'

"'My son,' the father said, 'you are always with me, and everything I have is yours. But we had to celebrate and be glad, because this brother of yours was dead and is alive again; he was lost and is found.'"

CLOSER THAN YOU'D THINK

EVEN AFTER ALL these years, there's no doubt about the grandeur of ancient Bet She'an. It wasn't as metropolitan as Caesarea, but the ruins leave no doubt. Bet She'an was one of the best little cities Alexander the Great planted in the Middle East roughly 2,200 years ago.

If you could go back and walk the paved streets of Bet She'an, you would see a city as "modern" as anything you could find in America in the early 1900s. The paving stones were smooth and level. A city water and sewer system lay beneath the streets. A state-of-the-art, picturesque theater was cut into a hillside. Strong columns, exquisite in their beauty, were everywhere. As one of the Greek cities of the Decapolis, Bet She'an would have also been home to a gymnasium, temples to pagan gods, and a way of life that was shockingly different from religious Judaism.

It will work best if you could picture the neon lights of Las Vegas flashing over the buildings of Bet She'an. Put a few dancing girls on site, add a brothel or two, and try to imagine a community philosophy that threw off all the restraints of old-fashioned, religious morality. The smell of roasting pork filled the air, and the idea that human beings were the center of the universe challenged the mind. Bet She'an may not have been the wildest little city in the Decapolis, but to the ultra conservative Jews scattered all around the Sea of Galilee, it was shockingly wicked. To those who visited the place? Let's just say, "What happens in Bet She'an, stays in Bet She'an."

Alexander the Great's philosophy of conquest was one of the most polite—and most effective—ever devised. He didn't force Greek Hellenism on the people he ruled. He simply had new Greek cities built in the conquered land, and invited people to try a new way of living. It was a tempting offer.

The "Decapolis" was originally a cluster of ten cities planted in what we now know as Jordan and Israel. True to form, Hellenism proved to be so popular that there were soon more than ten. According to some sources, they almost doubled in number!

In stark contrast to the brand-new, Hellenistic communities was the Orthodox Jewish community in Israel. Perhaps one of the most conservative corners of the entire land was scattered along the northern shoreline of the Sea of Galilee. If you've read the story of Jesus in the Bible, you'll recognize some of the names: Magdala, Bethsaida, Chorazin, and Capernaum. Not far from Capernaum, Jesus' adopted hometown, was Gamla. The inhabitants of Gamla were so fiercely committed to the Jewish life that thousands would eventually choose death rather than be subject to Roman rule. While Alexander and the Greeks *offered* a new way of life in the Decapolis, the Romans weren't nearly so gentle after they took over the land.

But before Gamla fell, and before Roman soldiers made Jewish blood run like water forty years after Jesus died, the Jewish rabbis repeatedly warned of the dangers of the Decapolis. It was such a foreign way of life on the other side of the lake, it was like a different world. They even gave the Decapolis a nickname. They called it "The Far Country."

That brings us to one of the most loved parables Jesus ever told. A father had two sons, Jesus said, and the younger of the two sons demanded his inheritance early. He then headed off . . . *"to a far country."*

If Jesus were telling this story in Capernaum, every head would have instinctively turned and looked across the lake. From Capernaum, it wasn't all that far to Hippos, perhaps the closest of the pagan cities. On a clear night, they might have seen the lights. On their journeys to Jerusalem, they would have passed by Bet She'an. Some probably purchased food there. More than likely, they had heard stories about what it was like from people who'd been there. They'd been given explicit warnings from the rabbis not to even *think* about the ten sinful cities the Greeks had built. It was a different, dangerous world.

But they all knew Hippos and Bet She'an were right there. Although there were other such places, Hippos and Bet She'an were close enough to touch. In fact, if a father's rebellious son really wanted to visit either place, he could be there by nightfall.

The "Far Country," as it turns out, was closer than we thought.

It still is.

If a follower of Christ is tempted by the bright lights of Las Vegas, the drunkenness of Bourbon Street, the dancing girls at a nearby strip club, the casino riverboats on the Mississippi, or any and all of it, on the Internet he can be there as quickly as he wants. A plane can take you anywhere you'd like to be in a matter of hours. The Internet can take you there in seconds.

However, the Far Country is not a good place to be. If you know the story of the prodigal son, you know he came to his senses only after he lost his money and nearly starved to death. His vacation to the Land of the Forbidden turned into a disaster.

It's important to remember that this was a parable. It's a story. Jesus wasn't referring to any incident in particular, though it certainly wouldn't have surprised anyone if somewhere in the Jewish community, a teenaged boy who never had the forbidden pork, who'd never seen a girl even partially unclothed, had given in to lust and headed off for Alexander's playground.

This frightens us, because we all know the truth. The Far Country is closer than we ever thought it was.

There's another place closer than we ever thought it was, too.

Call it "Home."

As soon as the boy came to his senses, Jesus said, he realized that home was a very real option. His dad would give him a job, almost certainly. He would have food in his belly and a second chance at making something out of his life. It would be embarrassing, but it was a way to stay alive.

He never anticipated the grace his father would shower upon him. He never knew there would be a party to celebrate his homecoming, nor that it would be so boisterous that it would infuriate his older brother. The grace for this once lost, now found young man was amazing indeed.

But be careful not to think that this family in the parable would have lived happily ever after just because the prodigal came home.

In the culture of the day, the oldest son usually received twice the inheritance of any other children. It would be his responsibility to continue the family business, and therefore, he would get twice the resources for this purpose. If the parable Jesus told was true, the younger son in the story would have been out of resources. When the day came for an attorney to read the will, he would get nothing more than an heirloom or two. All the cash would go to Son No. 1.

In other words, the consequences of his choices would follow him the rest of his life as surely as they'll follow you. He'd fight an uphill battle to build a bank account. No doubt, there would be tension between the two siblings. For the older brother, forgiveness would be extremely hard to hand down, especially if it required writing an occasional check to help Son No. 2 out of a jam.

This is life as we know it. The "Far Country" is closer than ever. Ways to hurt yourself are seconds away. Ways to waste your money are waiting . . . *today*. Ways to destroy your health are all around you. Temptation, as the Bible calls it, is enjoying the strongest economy it has ever known. And if we go there, consequences will follow. Grace may throw us a party when we come back, but grace won't erase a pregnancy, restore a reputation, add years to a damaged body, or rebuild a bank account.

What stays in Bet She'an is usually ruined in Bet She'an. Don't go there at all. If you've been, never go back. If you're there right now . . .

Come home.

It's a rare person who hasn't played all the roles in the parable of the prodigal.

Start with the younger son. If you've ever chosen your own way, you've visited the "Far Country," just as he did. And if the people of Jesus' day thought the wicked places were close to them, they should see how close they are now! With the click of a computer mouse, any of us can be covered up in the sin of our choice in cyberspace. We can be in the "Far Country" in seconds. And additionally, all the pre-Internet-era temptations are still in effect, too. Are you playing the part of the younger son today? Have you been jolted at how bad life can be when you've made the wrong choices? Come home. Grace is always waiting, but the first move is up to you.

Or what of the older brother? Do you know someone who keeps "getting away with murder"? Is it hard to accept how lavish the grace of the Father can be? This is tough, but it's a must if mature discipleship is to be had. We must let God deal with the choices other people make in his own way. The job of being God belongs only to God. If we cast judgment on another, we've cast judgment upon ourselves. Jesus did not mince words. "Do not judge, or you too will be judged," he said in the Sermon on the Mount (Matthew 7:1). To illustrate this, he offered the ridiculous picture of someone offering to help take a speck of dust out of someone else's eye . . . when all the time there was a log in his own eye! If you are playing the part of the older brother today, maybe it all boils down to a question of love. Do you love the same people God loves? Can you forgive when forgiveness is called for, and actually rejoice when someone bathes in grace? Even if it costs you part of your inheritance?

And finally, there is the Father, horribly disappointed in the choices his younger son has made. And yet he waits, looking for the first opportunity to race down the road and embrace his broken child. Are you waiting today? Has someone you love made the kind of choices that have left you standing in the doorway of a relationship, hoping the prodigal will come to his or her senses? Keep waiting. Model the patience of the One who told this story. Model his love. And keep praying for your prodigal.

JUDGES 15:11–12

Then three thousand men from Judah went down to the cave in the rock of Etam and said to Samson, "Don't you realize that the Philistines are rulers over us? What have you done to us?"

He answered, "I merely did to them what they did to me."

They said to him, "We've come to tie you up and hand you over to the Philistines."

1 SAMUEL 22:1–2

David left Gath and escaped to the cave of Adullam. When his brothers and his father's household heard about it, they went down to him there. All those who were in distress or in debt or discontented gathered around him, and he became their leader. About four hundred men were with him.

NO LONE RANGERS
ALLOWED

BACK WHEN THE WORLD was black and white, the Lone Ranger was one popular dude.

He appeared in 1933, seen only in the imaginations of millions of adults and children who listened to his exploits on the radio. Once he found television, the masked stranger and his white steed found an even larger audience, riding into story after story, saving the day every single time. It helped to have a white horse. Television shows were first broadcast without color and certainly without anything close to "high definition." There was a shade of gray to everything except the difference between right and wrong. The Lone Ranger was always on the right side of right.

"Who was that masked man?" someone would invariably ask as they watched the hero riding Silver into the sunset. To answer the question, Tonto might identify him as "Kemo Sabe," the "trusted friend." Bad guys referred to him as their mortal enemy, though they all seemed to understand the justice he handed out. You? You know the truth. He's a comic-book hero. He's a figment of Hollywood's imagination. He's a long, long way from reality.

For there is no such thing as a Lone Ranger.

There's always a Tonto. There are always others who know him, who feed him, who encourage him. There are even enemies who taunt him. But the simplest truth is the most obvious. He's not alone. He's in community.

The Bible's version of the Lone Ranger was a bodybuilder named Samson. Born to godly parents in the foothills southwest of modern-day Jerusalem, Samson was born miraculously, appointed by God to lead his people, and set aside for a life of holiness. His hair was not to be cut, he was not to drink wine, and not to eat anything unclean. He was a man born to be godly.

If you know the story (it runs from Judges 13–16), Samson was an expert at growing hair, but perhaps the worst example of a holy man the Bible has ever seen. He once ate honey out of a dead lion—a clear violation of Jewish law, and a distasteful thing to do in any culture. He found the Philistine version of Bourbon Street and visited there often. He loved a good fight, wasn't afraid to kill, and he had a weak spot for forbidden women. By the time Delilah arranged for his first haircut, Samson had long since cut off any semblance of holiness.

He was also one more thing. Samson was a Lone Ranger.

Samson didn't need help from the men of Judah. In one battle, he killed hundreds with the jawbone of a donkey, all by himself. If the rest of his people were afraid to face the Philistines, Samson certainly was not. He went solo time after time after time.

However, the downside of fighting alone was—let's find the perfect way to say this here—*being alone*.

After one of his many fights, Samson took cover in a cave. Naturally, he was alone. Company came calling. Three thousand men from Judah came down to the foothills, found Samson in his hideout, and had a conversation with the wild man.

Kemo Sabe they were not!

They complained bitterly about Samson's most recent exploits, and then—very carefully—asked permission to turn their local "Lone Ranger" over to the enemy. They tied him up, handed him over, and then watched in shock as Samson killed a thousand more Philistines.

As you probably know, Samson kept flirting with danger until he lost his hair, his power, and his eyes. Though he killed another few thousand Philistines as he died, his entire term as "leader" of Israel was a sad story of missed opportunity. He missed his chance to reach his God-given potential. The people missed their chance to have a godly, super-strong leader who could have made their lives better.

Funny thing about the cave Samson hid in. It's not all that far from another cave the Bible tells us about. The caves of Adullam are a maze of underground wonders and are within walking distance of the area where Samson lived. You can explore them, sing in them (the acoustics are fantastic), or hide there.

David hid in one of the caves of Adullam, just one healthy hike from Samson's cave. Both caves were in the same general vicinity. And like Samson, David was alone when he reached his cave.

David had been a giant killer as a young teen. He was told he was going to be the next king by Samuel the famous prophet. But soon, he was Israel's most

wanted man. King Saul did not like the competition David offered him, so his armies chased David across Israel. He traveled from hiding place to hiding place, often fighting with Samson-like results.

But unlike Samson, David was no Lone Ranger.

Hardly ever will you find David by himself. Thinking ahead to his encounter with Bathsheba, he probably didn't *need* to be alone. Neither do we, but that's a lesson for another day. For now, just know that David despised loneliness.

More than once he wrote songs decrying his sensation of being alone. He didn't want to be separated from God, and he didn't want to be separated from people. Once, when the Bible tells us he was "in the cave," he came up with these words:

> *Look to my right and see;*
> *no one is concerned for me.*
> *I have no refuge;*
> *no one cares for my life. (Psalm 142:4)*

Was he in one of the caves of Adullam when he wrote that? No one knows. Doesn't even matter. A cave is a cave is a cave. You get in one, it's tough. It's lonely in there. There's no daylight. It's musty. It's a fine place to explore on a short expedition, but don't try living there without some other cave dwellers.

Thankfully, David didn't have to stay in the cave of Adullam by himself for very long.

David left Gath and escaped to the cave of Adullam. When his brothers and his father's household heard about it, they went down to him there. All those who were in distress or in debt or discontented gathered around him, and he became their leader. About four hundred men were with him. (1 Samuel 22:1–2)

So get the picture. Two caves in the same general vicinity, and two men chosen by God to lead their people. One man is tied up and rejected by his community, and the other is surrounded by support. Admittedly, the men who came to join David weren't the "A" team. They were "in distress, or in debt, or discontented"! Nevertheless, David wasn't alone. In a relatively short period of time he became king, and as of today, he's still considered the greatest king in Israel's history.

Could the difference between success and failure of a leader depend on the support he or she has from a team? Could community be that important?

You know it is. We were not designed to be Lone Rangers. We were designed for community.

So find a friend. Reconnect. Be a friend. Make a new one. Tonto had it right. Even the Lone Ranger wasn't alone. Even he had a trusted friend. Tonto was a faithful companion. He was Kemo Sabe, and you can be, too.

First, spend some time thinking about the friends God has given you. Make sure today is a day you really comprehend the value of having a buddy, a confidant, a sister, a brother, a Kemo Sabe. They have helped you develop to this point, and if you take advantage of their friendship, they can help you maximize your God-given potential.

And second, look around your circle of influence today. There may very well be someone within your line of sight who's in a cave of sorts. Find her. Speak to him. Come to that "cave dweller" the way people came to David. No, you probably aren't the perfect person with all the right resources. But David didn't get the first-stringers, either. Just go. Be a friend. Speak the kind word. Encourage.

You might just have a hand in creating the next great leader for God's people!

Want to go deeper with this lesson? Read the background passages surrounding these key verses. Judges 15 has Samson's story, and Psalm 142 provides a good look at David's heart when he was "in the cave."

I will extol the LORD at all times;
    his praise will always be on my lips.
My soul will boast in the LORD;
    let the afflicted hear and rejoice.
Glorify the LORD with me;
    let us exalt his name together.
I sought the LORD, and he answered me;
    he delivered me from all my fears.
Those who look to him are radiant;
    their faces are never covered with shame.
This poor man called, and the LORD heard him;
    he saved him out of all his troubles.
The angel of the LORD encamps around those who fear him,
    and he delivers them.
Taste and see that the LORD is good;
    blessed is the man who takes refuge in him.
Fear the LORD, you his saints,
    for those who fear him lack nothing.
The lions may grow weak and hungry,
    but those who seek the LORD lack no good thing.
Come, my children, listen to me;
    I will teach you the fear of the LORD.

Whoever of you loves life
and desires to see many good days,
keep your tongue from evil
and your lips from speaking lies.
Turn from evil and do good;
seek peace and pursue it.
The eyes of the LORD are on the righteous
and his ears are attentive to their cry;
the face of the LORD is against those who do evil,
to cut off the memory of them from the earth.
The righteous cry out, and the LORD hears them;
he delivers them from all their troubles.
The LORD is close to the brokenhearted
and saves those who are crushed in spirit.
A righteous man may have many troubles,
but the LORD delivers him from them all;
he protects all his bones,
not one of them will be broken.
Evil will slay the wicked;
the foes of the righteous will be condemned.
The LORD redeems his servants;
no one will be condemned who takes refuge in him.

WHERE THE
GIANTS FALL

SOME GIANTS ARE nine feet tall, carry weapons, and shout curses in the Valley.

You surely know the Bible's story. Goliath was massive in size, trained for battle, and armed to the teeth. This was the giant David faced when he was only thirteen or so, in the grand theater of the Elah Valley.

But Goliath was not the last oversized enemy David faced, or even his toughest nemesis. In time, David would return to the very valley where Goliath had taken a shot to the head, where a battle had turned on one boy's courage. But on his second trip to the Valley of Elah, David was older, wiser, and smarting from an expensive lesson he had just learned. By then, he knew what we all have to learn.

There simply will never be a shortage of giants we have to fight.

Go to the Elah Valley today, and you'll not find much more than a small gas station that stands watch over the Elah Junction. The two roads that meet there are lightly traveled, and few people stop to consider David's story. Indeed, there's not even a historical marker set up to mark the spot.

But the Bible tells us this little intersection was quite the place three thousand years ago.

Most of the valleys in the rolling hills below Jerusalem run north and south. But a handful run east and west, and the Elah Valley is one of them. When the ancient armies of Judah and the Philistines met in battle, they naturally chose the valleys that gave them the straightest approach to one another. In the most famous of those epic battles, the Bible very clearly tells us that the Elah Valley was riveted with tension.

Now the Philistines gathered their forces for war and assembled at Socoh in Judah. They pitched camp at Ephes Dammim, between Socoh and Azekah. Saul and the Israelites assembled and camped in the Valley of Elah and drew up their battle line to meet the Philistines. The Philistines occupied one hill and the Israelites another, with the valley between them. (1 Samuel 17:1–3)

It was in this setting where Goliath defied the armies of the Living God, and where the armies of the Living God cowered on the hillside. With the recent discovery of what archeologists are calling the "Elah Fortress," they may have even been protected by city walls. That might help explain the "siege" atmosphere that preceded David's famous fight. For forty days, the Bible says, the giant Goliath came to the center of the valley and made his terrifying and insulting speeches. He challenged Judah to send a man against him so the fight could be settled in a one-on-one, battle-to-the-death contest.

No such man came from the ranks of Judah's army. They only listened to the tirade, day after day after day. But when a ruddy-faced boy named David came to the valley, everything changed.

David courageously charged at Goliath, holding tightly to a small slingshot and a really big faith. He fired only one stone, but when it hit Goliath in a perfect spot, the big man crumpled to the ground. David used Goliath's own sword—and it must have seemed as big as David himself—to cut off the giant's head.

From there, the battle turned quickly, and David became what we might call a "rock star." He had fans from one end of the country to the other, with the big exception of jealous king Saul who'd been shown up in the Valley of Elah.

I wonder if David thought his battle against giants was over.

There's never just one giant.

Of course, not every giant dresses up like Goliath. If Goliath shows up, it's pretty easy to spot the enemy. He's wearing armor, he's got a shield, a sword, an armor bearer, and he's stunningly strong. He announces his presence, he wears the uniform of an enemy, and his business card is printed with the blood of his victims.

Other giants arrive in disguise.

Take fear, for one. Or anxiety. Stress is another, and loneliness is a real killer. They are partners in crime, and they run in the same circles.

In time, the giants of fear, anxiety, stress, and loneliness came closer to killing David than Goliath ever did.

Add a decade to David's life, and you'll get a much taller and stronger man. If you know his story, you'll also know that by the time he was twenty, David was a fugitive. Saul, the king, wanted David dead. So David had run from one cave to the next, from one end of Israel to the other, and managed to avoid capture or execution.

But it was wearing on him, and there were times when he was exhausted, hungry, and alone.

Take the time when he and a very small group of men came to the priests of Nob. According to 1 Samuel 21, David and his men come alone, eat the sacred food, and discover the sword of Goliath. David took the sword, separated from his men, and went to a fortress called Gath.

That's an important detail.

Don't miss this. Gath was a Philistine fortress. It guarded the entire coastal plain that had been home to Philistine communities for centuries. What's more, Gath was the hometown of Goliath, the very giant David had killed in the Elah Valley several years before.

Carrying Goliath's sword, David swaggered into Gath. Why did he go there? We're not sure. He was probably looking for work. He was a professional soldier, and in the years before he became king, he often worked security for whoever hired him.

But this time, he met new giants in Gath.

It started when he heard people talking about him. There was a buzz in Gath about the giant killer.

> *That day David fled from Saul and went to Achish king of Gath. But the servants of Achish said to him, "Isn't this David, the king of the land? Isn't he the one they sing about in their dances:*
>
> *"'Saul has slain his thousands,*
> *and David his tens of thousands'?" (1 Samuel 21:10–11)*

David had a panic attack. He became afraid, the Bible tells us. Instead of looking for work, he began looking for a way out. He became convinced that the entire city wanted revenge, and that King Achish would take him prisoner.

His plan of survival? Let's just say it wasn't pretty.

> *David took these words to heart and was very much afraid*
> *of Achish king of Gath. So he pretended to be insane in their*
> *presence; and while he was in their hands he acted like a*
> *madman, making marks on the doors of the gate and letting*
> *saliva run down his beard. (1 Samuel 21:12–13)*

Ironically, it worked. The king announced that he had plenty of madmen already, and that he wanted David out of Gath.

So David left Gath, cleaned himself up, and took stock of his life. He also walked to the caves of Adullam. That's the first detail from 1 Samuel 22, and perhaps the writer of this story assumed we'd know where the caves of Adullam were.

But maybe you don't. These are some of the "secrets" still hidden in plain sight in Israel today.

The caves of Adullam are tucked under the same hills that make up the Valley of Elah, just six miles or so from Gath. To get to the caves, David had to walk through the very valley where he'd beaten Goliath.

He must have remembered the day he stepped out in faith and took down the giant.

Goliath was cursing God, cursing God's armies, and when he saw David, he started cursing the boy.

> *Am I a dog, that you come against with me with sticks?*
> *(1 Samuel 17:43)*

But David just kept moving forward, swinging his slingshot, and pronouncing his faith in the living God.

> David said to the Philistine, "You come against me with sword and spear and javelin, but I come against you in the name of the LORD Almighty, the God of the armies of Israel, whom you have defied. This day the LORD will hand you over to me, and I'll strike you down and cut off your head. Today I will give the carcasses of the Philistine army to the birds of the air and the beasts of the earth, and the whole world will know that there is a God in Israel. All those gathered here will know that it is not by sword or spear that the LORD saves; for the battle is the LORD's, and he will give all of you into our hands." (1 Samuel 17:45–47)

Sure enough, the giant fell, the Philistines ran, and David was an instant hero. His speech would be quoted all over Israel, and people took pride in the young man with a giant-sized faith.

But now a few years had passed. Time and stress had worn on him. He was no longer the innocent boy trusting that God would rescue him in every situation, if he'd only have enough faith to charge the enemy.

How could he have not remembered his battle with Goliath as he walked through the battlefield? And how could he have not reflected on how far he had fallen from that courageous faith? Had he really just spent several days clawing a city gate and letting spit decorate his beard? Had he really just depended on an insanity act as his plan of salvation?

He might have been in possession of Goliath's sword, but he didn't possess the swagger any longer.

Some new giants had gotten the better of him.

David had met Fear in Gath. He had taken a shot to the gut from Anxiety, and Loneliness had sucker-punched him from behind. Fearsome giants, all of them.

In comparison, Goliath had been child's play. David's new enemies took no prisoners.

But as he escaped from Gath and walked through the Valley of Elah, David remembered the basics. He had no reason to fear the people of Gath. In reality, they were in awe of David, the giant killer. The sight of Goliath's own sword strapped on David's waist left no doubt to the young man's ability to fight.

In reality, Achish the king of Gath never put David behind bars. No one handcuffed him. There were never any chains on his feet.

David had been imprisoned only by his own fears. Stress had taken him down for the count, and there wasn't a friendly face in sight.

But in the Valley of Elah, David made a decision. He would never, ever go back to faking

insanity again. Fear would not win any more battles. Stress would be controlled. Anxiety would have to wait.

He penned and sang the words we know as Psalm 34. We know he did this because of the notation David included with the song. The word *Abimelech*, by the way, means "king." The king's name was Achish.

> *I will extol the LORD at all times;*
>   *his praise will always be on my lips.*
> *My soul will boast in the LORD;*
>   *let the afflicted hear and rejoice.*
> *Glorify the LORD with me;*
>   *let us exalt his name together.*
> *I sought the LORD, and he answered me;*
>   *he delivered me from all my fears. (Psalm 34:1–4)*

Do you hear it? "Never again will I give in to fear. The Lord has rescued me before, and the Lord will rescue me from now on. It was the Lord who allowed me to take down the first giant, and it will be the Lord who helps me beat the giants yet to come."

The Lord delivered David.

Not from facing future giants, but from fear. Not from future problems, but from anxiety. Not from future battles, but from stress.

Even loneliness was about to fall.

David left Gath and escaped to the cave of Adullam. When his brothers and his father's household heard about it, they went down to him there. . . . About four hundred men were with him. (1 Samuel 22:1–2)

There's a critically important lesson here. For David, Gath was the wrong place. For David, being alone was a dangerous life situation. If you'll remember, the next time we are told David is alone, his eyes find Bathsheba, and the worst chapter of his life begins. For David, when stress and fear and imagined anxieties build up, it proves too much to bear.

None of that is unique to David.

God will not spare us the battles of life. David had Goliath. You might have a debilitating illness. David had Gath. You might find yourself in a frightening place, too. David had his stress points, and you'll have yours. David had been worn thin by Saul's pursuit. You might have debt collectors calling at all hours of the day.

The Lord is still the God of the giant-killers.

David learned his lesson in Gath. He rebounded, refocused, and soon became king over all Israel. He is still revered as the greatest king the country ever knew. He did it with the support of his community, and with a determination that he would trust in the Lord with all his heart, soul, mind, and strength as he went into battle.

Got a giant? Face it head-on. Discover that God still delivers us from our fears.

There's an interesting thing about David's reign as king. One of the cities he wasted no time before conquering? Gath. He returned with an army, and took the fortress where he'd intentionally made himself look foolish.

Apparently, David didn't want anyone in Gath to remember the "madman" in their midst.

Has fear ever made you look foolish? Have you ever worried about something that proved to be nothing to worry about? Has anxiety ever worn you down, made you sick, or kept you up at night?

Put yourself in David's sandals and memorize Psalm 34. Try to envision what it was like for him to return to the Valley of Elah and vow to never give in to fear again. More passages for you to memorize to help you battle fear could include David's proclamation to Goliath as he moved toward the giant (1 Samuel

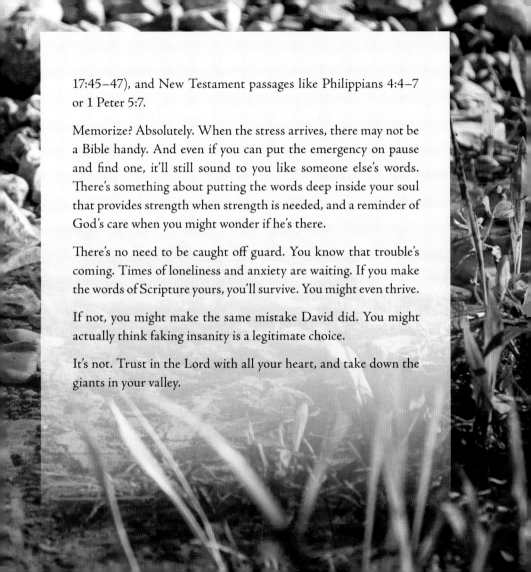

17:45–47), and New Testament passages like Philippians 4:4–7 or 1 Peter 5:7.

Memorize? Absolutely. When the stress arrives, there may not be a Bible handy. And even if you can put the emergency on pause and find one, it'll still sound to you like someone else's words. There's something about putting the words deep inside your soul that provides strength when strength is needed, and a reminder of God's care when you might wonder if he's there.

There's no need to be caught off guard. You know that trouble's coming. Times of loneliness and anxiety are waiting. If you make the words of Scripture yours, you'll survive. You might even thrive.

If not, you might make the same mistake David did. You might actually think faking insanity is a legitimate choice.

It's not. Trust in the Lord with all your heart, and take down the giants in your valley.

Now there was a man in Jerusalem called Simeon, who was righteous and devout. He was waiting for the consolation of Israel, and the Holy Spirit was upon him. It had been revealed to him by the Holy Spirit that he would not die before he had seen the Lord's Christ. Moved by the Spirit, he went into the temple courts. When the parents brought in the child Jesus to do for him what the custom of the Law required, Simeon took him in his arms and praised God, saying:

> "Sovereign Lord, as you have promised,
>> you now dismiss your servant in peace.
> For my eyes have seen your salvation,
>> which you have prepared in the sight of all people, a light for
>> revelation to the Gentiles
>> and for glory to your people Israel."

The child's father and mother marveled at what was said about him. Then Simeon blessed them and said to Mary, his mother: "This child is destined to cause the falling and rising of many in Israel, and to be a sign that will be spoken against, so that the thoughts of many hearts will be revealed. And a sword will pierce your own soul too."

THERE IS NO
FREE PASS

I T WAS A WEEK BEFORE Mother's Day, 2009.

It was also just one day after the baby shower at their church. Amy and Brad Von Oven were waiting on the birth of their fourth child when something went horribly and instantly wrong. Bethany Hope died just before she was born, and Amy and Brad were thrown into the worst grief they had ever imagined.

It would take months for them to work through their anguish, and as long as they live, they will never forget the day when their hearts were broken in Labor and Delivery.

It was a contradiction in logic. Amy and Brad were committed followers of Christ. They were a fixture at their church, and leaders among the young adults. They had paid their dues, if God needs dues, and done their time, if you get credit for attending church services.

Why would God allow such pain to one of his best young couples? Shouldn't faithfulness lead to a life that *at least* doesn't include Sunday mornings of gut-wrenching loss?

Her name was Mary, and if anyone should have gotten a free pass from pain, she was that person. Chosen by God to be the mother of the Messiah, Mary was obviously a faithful young woman. She had paid all the dues, passed all the tests, and was found to be something close to perfect in the eyes of her God.

But right from the start, Mary had a difficult time.

She was too young for such a big job, but God gave it to her anyway.

She was completely inexperienced. She couldn't afford to make a mistake, for Child No. 1 would be the most important baby in history. God chose her, anyway.

She was from no important place, no prestigious family, and she had nothing that would indicate to outsiders that she was special among all women. But God still asked her to take on the most important parenting role the world had ever known.

Mary chose to obey, and God immediately allowed her reputation to be trashed.

One of her first instructions was to find her older relative Elizabeth, who lived in a suburb of Jerusalem. She made the long trip, almost certainly *walking* the ninety or so miles, probably dealing with the first few days of morning sickness while she traveled. She returned three months later, while it was still fairly easy for her to travel. But as you surely know, she had to make another trip to the most famous suburb of Jerusalem when she was full-term. She and Joseph reached Bethlehem just in time for the baby to be born in a shepherd's cave, where a feed trough would serve as a baby bed.

And that was just the pregnancy.

After the baby was born, there was a terror-framed race to Egypt, and a frightening trip under the radar back to Nazareth, where she finally introduced her little boy to her own mother.

Somewhere along the way, Joseph died. At least we think that's what happened to him. All we know is that he was with Mary when Jesus was twelve, and he wasn't there when Jesus was thirty. He was the love of her life, the one person who would not turn his back on her . . . and then he was gone.

The truth of her life? Though there must have been much joy and laughter, there were also days that left her as crushed with grief as anyone who's ever known the pain of loss.

But the sword that would ultimately pierce her heart was still in its sheath. The old man at the temple had promised it when the baby was just eight days old, and no matter how she must have tried to forget his words, she must have wondered what they meant.

Simeon had blessed the child, thanked God for the promise fulfilled, and then looked at the young girl who'd agreed to take on the world's most important job of mothering. "And a sword will pierce your own soul too."

This was the blessing of God upon his obedient servant?

Mary was so faithful to God. She attended Passover every year, in Jerusalem. She was there when Jesus was twelve. She was there again when he was thirty-three. Perhaps there were years when a newborn kept her home, but for most of her life, she made the very long trip for the holy day simply because God's Word commanded it.

One of those trips stood out above all the others because of its sheer horror. She was approaching fifty that Passover, and as she made the journey to Jerusalem, she had no idea what awaited her son. In the blink of an eye, it seemed, he went from a Passover hero to a condemned man. He was beaten nearly to death, stripped of his clothes, practically stripped of his skin, and then stuck on a stick and left to writhe in agony for six hours just outside the city gates.

She was there, at the foot of the cross, as he bled to death. She was there as the skies turned black, as the earth shook and as people screamed in terror. Some might have been afraid the world was ending. She was convinced it had.

She must have held him as he was lowered from the cross, arms still extended, nearly frozen with rigor mortis. Since he had quoted the first line of Psalm 22, she deserved an answer to the question, too. Why had God forsaken her? Why so much pain? Of *all* people, shouldn't the mother of the Christ get a free pass from this kind of pain?

There is no free pass. If you live long enough, pain will invade your heart. Heartache and grief and depression and despair are part of the life experience, even if you're one of God's greatest servants.

On that dark and painful day, Mary couldn't have known some of the things we know about her life.

We know that God was in complete control, even if she felt completely out of control. We know that the cross wasn't the end of the story. Instead, it was the necessary conclusion of centuries of preparation, a fulfillment to prophecy and a payment for sin, for anyone wise enough to accept the grace.

We also know something else about this life. I wonder if Mary struggled with this inescapable truth as much as we struggle with it.

That truth? It had never been about her in the first place.

It's funny. We spend all of our lives looking in mirrors, wondering how the world perceives us, wondering if things are going to work out the way we'd like them to work out. In truth, it was never about us at all. The world doesn't revolve around us any more than it revolves around a single ant on a single anthill in a world filled with too many anthills to count. There are billions of us alive right now, and billions more that have lived before us. Unless God calls an end to the timeline, there will be billions more that follow us.

And it was never about any of us.

To God alone belongs the glory. To Him alone belongs all praise, all power, and all focus. We call him "Lord," which means "Boss." More than that, actually. He is our Commander. He is in charge, and his commands are unquestioned. He is the owner, and we are those who are owned. If he gives an order, we obey it. It matters not what happens as a result of that obedience. It matters only that we obey.

There were times when Mary was hurting too much to see it, but the truth is, God used her to change the world. Her obedience was a gift to God . . . and a gift to us.

Here's the good news about Mary. Since she was in Jerusalem for the crucifixion, she was also there on Sunday. She was an eyewitness to the empty tomb! She had a chance, finally, to understand what had happened. The pain she had known had a purpose. The stunning news of Sunday morning's resurrection didn't take away the nightmare of Friday, but because of the resurrection, nothing would *ever* take away her joy!

There will come a day, if you are a follower of Christ, when you shall have a fresh perspective of joy. If not here, in this lifetime, then it will come the instant you taste the joy of eternity.

To believe this truth is the very definition of faith.

And to obey the God who will allow you to suffer, is the very definition of love.

Love him today.

No matter what.

Can you obey God on the bad days, as well as the good?

Remember Amy and Brad? In time, Amy wrote a short book about her pain as a way to help other mothers who suffered the loss of a child at birth. A few weeks after the funeral, Brad shared their story with his church, and sang as if God had been amazingly good to him during the entire ordeal. They have shared their story many times since that day, helping countless couples who have known the same sharp pains of stillborn births.

You may not be a writer or a singer. But each one of us has the ability to obey God, no matter what he asks of us, and no matter what he allows to happen.

When the day of pain pierces your soul, as it did for Mary, remember this: Most of your life will be filled with good days, and plenty of reasons to praise God. There won't be many days when you will have the opportunity to praise God when your heart is broken. But on that day, your praise—your obedience—will be a gift rarely given.

Don't miss that opportunity.

Love him. Trust him. Obey him.

No matter what.

Therefore everyone who hears these words of mine and puts them into practice is like a wise man who built his house on the rock. The rain came down, the streams rose, and the winds blew and beat against that house; yet it did not fall, because it had its foundation on the rock. But everyone who hears these words of mine and does not put them into practice is like a foolish man who built his house on sand. The rain came down, the streams rose, and the winds blew and beat against that house, and it fell with a great crash.

ONLY A FOOL . . .

IF YOU'RE LOOKING for a vacation at the beach, Israel probably isn't your place. The land Jesus knew didn't feature sandy beaches on either the Mediterranean coast or on the shores of the Sea of Galilee.

Instead of stretches of sand, there are layers of rocks.

Sharp rocks. Fist-sized, pain-inducing rocks.

The rocks are especially sharp around the Sea of Galilee, where Jesus did most of his ministry. Go swimming there, and you'll have new insight as to why Jesus chose to walk *on top* of the water. It simply hurts too much to walk on the bottom!

The land Jesus knew is dominated by rock. The farmers in Israel battled rocks in their fields every planting season. No matter how many times they had cleared the rocks from the fields, the winter rains would wash away the dirt and uncover a new crop of stones.

From the cliffs and mountains of the north to the rugged Negev in the south, Israel is one of the rockiest places on earth. Around Capernaum and Korazin, black basalt stone dominates. Jerusalem is built almost completely from light-colored limestone. There's little wonder why the ruins of Israel have survived. Almost every structure was built of stone, the most abundant natural resource of the country.

Which brings us back to sand.

There simply isn't a lot of sand in Israel.

There is one place, however, where you can find lots of sand.

Just south of Jericho, where countless travelers have turned west and started the hard climb toward Jerusalem, the dramatic cliffs of the Judean Wilderness line the shoreline of the Dead Sea.

The Dead Sea is the lowest place on earth, some 1,300 feet below sea level. Jerusalem lies atop the ridge of the Judean Mountains, 2,500 feet above sea level.

Since it's no more than twenty miles from the Judean Mountains to the Dead Sea, the land between those two points is some of the most dramatic you'll find anywhere.

There are no villages between the two points. There are barely any trees, and the ones you find aren't going to be very tall. There is some grass for a short season every spring, but most of the year, the Judean Wilderness looks like a dangerous, forsaken, very rocky land. The canyons of the land—called "wadis"—are dry riverbeds from streams that have cut deep, winding paths through the rocks for centuries.

And at the mouth of the wadis, you'll find sand. Lots of sand.

The cause of the sand's existence is simple to understand as a result of weather patterns and land elevation. It rarely rains over the area around the Dead Sea. Instead, the clouds roll in from the west, picking up their water over the Mediterranean, and dropping that water as they rise toward the ridgeline of the Judean Mountains, where Jerusalem and Bethlehem are perched. By the time the weather system passes Jerusalem, the clouds have been emptied of all their life-giving water.

People who raise crops and flocks on the western side of the ridgeline have enough water for a year. If the rainwater trickles off to the west, it simply adds to the bountiful living. Rainwater that trickles to the east of Jerusalem, however, finds the dry riverbeds around the city and turns those wadis into flowing streams. Deeper gullies follow, and the water gains speed and volume

as the gullies meet and the land falls dramatically toward the Dead Sea. Instead of soaking into the ground, the water rushes along the rocks, growing wilder and deeper with every passing mile.

By the time a wadi flood hits the narrow canyons at the end of its rushing journey, a wall of water might be thirty feet high, and it will be traveling at a very high rate of speed. It is not unusual to see cars, rocks, trees, and debris carried along by the flash flood.

It is also not uncommon for people to lose their lives in the raging torrent, for unless they know of the rain in Jerusalem fifteen or so miles away, their first warning of danger might be in the roaring sound of the first torrent of water racing through the canyons. If you hear it, you've only got a few seconds to reach higher ground. The success of your climb will be a matter of life or death.

The raging phenomenon of a wadi flood doesn't last very long. When the canyons suddenly open to the flat land of the Dead Sea area, the water quietly dissipates. Left behind?

Sand.

It is smooth, it is packed hard, and if you didn't know better, it might look like the perfect place to lay the foundation for a new home. If you're building a home anywhere else in Israel, you'll have to deal with the rocks. It'll take heavy equipment to lay a foundation in such land. In days gone by, when there were no giant machines to break through the rock, it must have been quite the struggle to build any structure.

But the sand? It's perfect. It's got ready-to-go characteristics. It's level, it's smooth, and it's deep.

But only a fool would build a home in the mouth of a wadi.

Not every wadi catches a flood every year, so it would be possible to build a house on the sand and *not* be immediately washed away. But sooner or later, any structure built in the mouth of a wadi would be swept away in a matter of seconds. Unless the residents got out in time, anyone living in the structure would probably be lost, too.

Which explains why there are no villages in the Judean Wilderness. It's too harsh during most of the year, and too dangerous during the short rainy season. No matter how difficult it might be to work with the rocks of Israel, it's just a much better idea to build your house somewhere else, somewhere on a solid-rock foundation. Build your house where the flash floods come, and your days are numbered.

According to Matthew's gospel, the conclusion of the Sermon on the Mount was a parable about home-building. Jesus spoke of a day when the rains would fall, the streams would rise, and the winds would blow and beat against a home.

A home built on the rock would stand. A home built on the sand—a home built in the mouth of a wadi—would fall!

No one argued with that statement. They only pictured the fool who would construct something so important, so expensive, in a place where it would soon be destroyed. It might rank as the worst decision a person could ever make.

And that's the point. The words Jesus gave are the words of life. To hear and obey them is a wise decision. To hear them and ignore them . . . is to invite certain destruction.

MAKE THE LESSON YOUR OWN

There are times when we hear the words of Jesus and become frightened by them. In the case of the parable of the wise and foolish builders, it's easy to wonder if, by chance, you'll be swept away by some coming destruction. The people who originally heard this teaching, though, would have known a different truth.

It would actually be much more difficult to complete the construction of a house on a sand foundation. Imagine the warnings that would come! Anyone seeing such construction would warn the builder of the coming danger. There would be undeniable evidence of past floods. There would be eyewitnesses of past destruction. In order to build a house on the sand—or in the mouth of a wadi—a builder would have to ignore warning after warning of the foolishness of his efforts.

Plus, there's hardly any sand in Israel, anyway! Most of the land is dominated by rock. To make a house-in-the-wadi mistake, you'd have to ignore almost all of your other options. Almost certainly, no one has ever built a house on Israel's sand! Homebuilders take warnings of coming destruction seriously.

Life-builders should do the same.

The point of the parable is to obey what Jesus teaches.

Before it can be obeyed, it must be heard.

Here are two challenges. First, take some time to read the Sermon on the Mount. It's Matthew 5, 6, and 7. It's the world's most famous sermon, given by the rabbi you probably claim to follow. If you want to make sure you've not built your life in the wrong place, the first step is to reacquaint yourself with the words.

The second challenge? Memorize the words.

You could choose a portion to memorize, like the Beatitudes (Matthew 5:1–11). You could memorize this parable of the wise and foolish builders. It's not very long. You could tackle a section of Jesus' teaching that has special meaning to you.

But the best thing to do is to memorize the entire thing. Something happens when we go beyond reading the words and put them in our hearts. We concentrate on phrases. We take a long time with the words. We reflect upon them. We have a much better chance of following the instructions, of doing what Jesus said to do, if we've got the words so close to our hearts. And in the tradition of Jesus and his followers, memorizing the words of Scripture is, in fact, part of the "doing."

Yes, it's hard work. It might even remind you of an ancient work of constructing a well-built home with a solid foundation.

But when the rains come and the streams rise, you'll be glad you went to the trouble.

But Jesus went to the Mount of Olives. At dawn he appeared again in the temple courts, where all the people gathered around him, and he sat down to teach them. The teachers of the law and the Pharisees brought in a woman caught in adultery. They made her stand before the group and said to Jesus, "Teacher, this woman was caught in the act of adultery. In the Law Moses commanded us to stone such women. Now what do you say?" They were using this question as a trap, in order to have a basis for accusing him.

But Jesus bent down and started to write on the ground with his finger. When they kept on questioning him, he straightened up and said to them, "If any one of you is without sin, let him be the first to throw a stone at her." Again he stooped down and wrote on the ground.

At this, those who heard began to go away one at a time, the older ones first, until only Jesus was left, with the woman still standing there. Jesus straightened up and asked her, "Woman, where are they? Has no one condemned you?"

"No one, sir," she said.

"Then neither do I condemn you," Jesus declared. "Go now and leave your life of sin."

JEREMIAH 17:13

O Lord, the hope of Israel,
 all who forsake you will be put to shame.
Those who turn away from you will be written in the dust
 because they have forsaken the Lord,
 the spring of living water.

WRITTEN IN
THE DUST

H E STOOD AT THE microphone, trying to find the right words.

Only problem was . . . there weren't any right words.

He'd been unfaithful to his wife, he'd gotten caught, and now he was in front of a bank of microphones. As a public official, his private choices had become the sharp focus of a Peeping-Tom public, and the news reporters were there to get every juicy detail.

The man looked like the successful politician he was. He was wearing an expensive suit. The press conference was being held in front of his office. He had a small team of aides nearby, though all of them were doing their best to stay out of camera range.

His career was in shambles, his legacy would always include mention of the scandal, and his marriage was on shaky ground.

He had been caught in the spider web of lust. Like a fly that couldn't escape, he would pay with his career for being in the wrong place at the wrong time.

His name? Doesn't matter. Read these words now, and you'll think of a recent case. Read them in another twenty years, and there will be a new scandal that comes to mind. Like flies in a spider's web, people like the ruined official have been getting caught in the web of lust for centuries. The pattern is not likely to change in the centuries to come.

It's the lure of the forbidden. The call of the wild. The temptation of the lover on the other side of the fence. The fact that it's an electric fence only charges the temptation with excitement.

And this is the irony of human nature. We all know the rules, and we all know people break them. Getting caught breaking them is the one thing a community simply will not forgive. In a sense, we say it this way: Keep a secret vice if you want. Just keep it a secret.

This has been true for centuries. One day, Jesus came face to face with a person who'd been caught in the embarrassing trap of lust. She was no politician. She wasn't even famous. She was just one more fly caught in one more web.

The story from John's gospel tells us only that she had been "caught in adultery." Instead of being surrounded by members of the media, she was surrounded by "teachers of the law and the Pharisees."

A couple of things come to mind here. For one, she's got an all-male audience. For another, she's probably not wearing much. If she was really caught in the very act, it's highly unlikely she was wearing her most conservative outfit. More than likely, she was lucky to grab a sheet. Her lack of clothing would have been good evidence to back up the charges. But even if she was fully dressed, even if she'd been held from the time of her affair until daylight, she would have felt naked. They would have seen through her clothes to the shame of her actions.

It was the worst moment of her life.

All the while, the flies who hadn't yet been caught were buzzing around her, shaking their heads at the most sexual thing they'd seen in a long time.

As you probably noticed, someone is missing from this scene. Where's the man in this story? She got caught, but her partner in crime is nowhere to be found. That's important, because the Law the vice squad was so intent on upholding required that both the man and the woman caught in adultery should be killed. The code can be found in Leviticus 20:10. You might need that reference, but they did not. They knew the Law by heart, which is why they were dragging this woman to a place where her sorry life could be eliminated from a community that deserved better.

They knew the Text. Remember that. It's important.

Jesus enters the story quite by accident. He was teaching in the temple when the important men and their sensuous prisoner interrupted everything.

"Teacher," they demanded, "this woman has been caught in adultery, in the very act. Now in the Law Moses commanded us to stone such women; what then do You say?" (John 8:4–5 NASB).

It was a trap. If Jesus cast a vote for grace, he'd be in direct violation of the Law. If he voted for the Law to be upheld, his popular message of grace would be negated.

Instead of answering the men, Jesus started writing on the ground, using his finger like a pen. The desert climate of the land means it's always dusty in Jerusalem. If you want to write your name on the ground, feel free. It won't be there later today, but you can write in the dust as surely as Jesus did.

They kept pressing him for an answer, but some of them had already realized what Jesus was doing. His writing in the dust *was* an answer.

Jesus stood up and gave the famous line: "If any one of you is without sin, let him be the first to throw a stone at her" (John 8:7).

And then he started writing in the dust again.

Some of the older ones took the opportunity to slip out. They had been around the Text longer than the younger ones. They had no intention of being the object of Jeremiah's blistering rebuke.

One by one they all left. When they were alone, Jesus sent the woman away, too. He told her she was free to go, but as she went, she was to "sin no more."

In our culture as we read this, the questions come fast and furious. What did Jesus write on the ground? What was he writing that was so convicting it caused all of the accusers to leave? Did he write their names, or the names of their secret lovers? Maybe a hotel room number that would embarrass one of the men? Did he write the Ten Commandments, perhaps? Inquiring minds want to know: *Jesus, what did you write?*

It's unlikely any of the people there that day gave whatever Jesus actually wrote much thought. Instead, they focused on the way they'd been trained. They reacted not the way *our* culture would react. They reacted the way *their* culture would react.

And their culture knew the Text.

From their first lessons at home through all of their formal schooling, and certainly through every time they'd heard the Scripture read in their synagogues, they'd known a simple truth.

The answer is in the Text. It's *always* in the Text.

This time, their minds would have searched for a case of someone writing in the dust.

That's why the older ones left first. They knew the words better than the younger ones. They had more time invested. They raced through the library of their mind faster than the rest, and remembered one of the most frightening visuals any of the prophets had ever painted.

Jeremiah, as angry as you'll ever see him, had announced that he was speaking for the Lord. The prophet told of a coming day when God would allow those who had hidden their sins to be fully punished. Jeremiah was speaking to the people of Jerusalem, of Judah. He spoke of the rich taking advantage of the poor. He warned a people who had not shown mercy to one another that they should not expect mercy from their God.

That was before the exile. That was before Jerusalem was sacked. That was before so many had been slaughtered, and before the theologians had discerned that all the terror had been a judgment of God.

Now that Jerusalem was again inhabited by God's people, Jeremiah's message was not the most popular sermon of the city. But in the same place where Jesus was now tracing in the dust, the ancient words still created fear.

"Those who turn away from God," Jeremiah had said, "will be written in the dust."

It's one thing for you and me to scratch out some words in the dirt. If the wind blows later today and the words disappear, no big deal. But if God writes a name in the dust? Now *that* carries serious implications. When a name disappears for eternity, all hope is lost.

Interesting, I think, that Jesus plays the role of God in this encounter. Just as interesting, he got away with it!

When the woman left, she'd been given grace, and given the clear understanding that she should now live her life like grace made a difference. No more sin. It was time for a turnaround.

And the story ends at that point, except for the epilogue.

You do know the conclusion, don't you?

If the religious police had actually carried through with their threat and stoned the woman, they wouldn't have stoned her on the temple grounds. Instead, they would have taken her to the place of execution. It was a logical choice, the same kind of choice cultures make today if they carry out an execution. There's a place, and there's a way. An execution without an accepted place and procedure is just another murder.

Jerusalem wasn't all that big of a place. Deep valleys bordered two sides of the city making it not conducive to heavy foot traffic. Executions couldn't have been held in either valley. The northeastern corner was too close to the Temple.

The northwestern corner of the city, however, had a spot where the stonecutters had finally run out of good rock. They had left a jagged looking cliff there, and folks said it looked like a human skull. Just outside a major city gate of Jerusalem, it was perfect for stoning. As for procedure, the convicted person would be taken to the top of the hill, forced to hear the evidence of their sin one more time, and then pushed off the cliff by his or her accusers. The stones would follow, although the guilty one would hope for a quick death after the fall. The ones who first brought the accusation would throw the first stones.

The woman Jesus rescued wasn't taken to that horrible cliff. Jesus had set her free. She didn't shed a drop of blood there.

But Jesus did go there.

The Romans thought Golgotha, the "place of the skull," was a perfect place for crucifixions. People were already scared of the place. It looked frightening. It already had the bloody reputation from previous executions, from previous stonings. They even liked the fact that it was in such a visible location. That served the Romans' philosophy of governing by fear very well.

So they followed their orders and executed the rabbi in the very place where the woman caught in adultery never had to go.

Remember the religious leaders who had asked Jesus whether he would choose grace for the woman, or whether he would choose to carry out the Law?

At Golgotha, they got their answer. He chose both.

She got the grace. He took her punishment.

And only sin was left written in the dust.

This story is rich in application opportunities.

Start by reading the words in Jeremiah 17. Read the entire chapter. Of course, you will read them from a Bible, whether it's printed on paper or showing up on an electronic screen. We have *lots* of Bibles. But remember that the people in Jerusalem that day had no personal copy of the Text. If they knew the words, they had memorized them. Here's another opportunity to do something Jesus did. Memorize a portion of Jeremiah's blistering rebuke—or even all of it.

Then, reflect on what happened at Golgotha—and on what did *not* happen there. It might help to read Romans 5:6–8. The man who wrote the words was Jewish, and extremely familiar with the place of execution. He had once stood there, overseeing the stoning of a man named Stephen. In time, he came to understand the power of grace, and the miracle of what had happened at Golgotha on Good Friday.

But perhaps the most important thing to do with this story is to put yourself in the place of the woman.

Perhaps you've even been there. Being caught in the act of sinning is a horrible experience.

Being set free from judgment is an answer to desperate prayer.

If Jesus were to tell you today that you were forgiven of your sin, but that he expected you to "go and sin no more," what would you be leaving behind?

Is there anything stopping you from leaving it behind today? Get it done.

Today.

Afterward Jesus appeared again to his disciples, by the Sea of Tiberias. It happened this way: Simon Peter, Thomas (called Didymus), Nathanael from Cana in Galilee, the sons of Zebedee, and two other disciples were together. "I'm going out to fish," Simon Peter told them, and they said, "We'll go with you." So they went out and got into the boat, but that night they caught nothing.

Early in the morning, Jesus stood on the shore, but the disciples did not realize that it was Jesus.

He called out to them, "Friends, haven't you any fish?"

"No," they answered.

He said, "Throw your net on the right side of the boat and you will find some." When they did, they were unable to haul the net in because of the large number of fish.

Then the disciple whom Jesus loved said to Peter, "It is the Lord!" As soon as Simon Peter heard him say, "It is the Lord," he wrapped his outer garment around him (for he had taken it off) and jumped into the water. The other disciples followed in the boat, towing the net full of fish, for they were not far from shore, about a hundred yards. When they landed, they saw a fire of burning coals there with fish on it, and some bread.

Jesus said to them, "Bring some of the fish you have just caught."

Simon Peter climbed aboard and dragged the net ashore. It was full of large fish, 153, but even with so many the net was not torn. Jesus said to them," Come and have breakfast." None of the disciples dared ask him, "Who are you?" They knew it was the Lord. Jesus came, took the bread and gave it to them, and did the same with the fish. This was now the third time Jesus appeared to his disciples after he was raised from the dead.

When they had finished eating, Jesus said to Simon Peter, "Simon son of John, do you truly love me more than these?"

"Yes, Lord," he said, "you know that I love you."

Jesus said, "Feed my lambs."

Again Jesus said, "Simon son of John, do you truly love me?"

He answered, "Yes, Lord, you know that I love you."

Jesus said, "Take care of my sheep."

The third time he said to him, "Simon son of John, do you love me?"

Peter was hurt because Jesus asked him the third time, "Do you love me?" He said, "Lord, you know all things; you know that I love you."

Jesus said, "Feed my sheep. I tell you the truth, when you were younger you dressed yourself and went where you wanted; but when you are old you will stretch out your hands, and someone else will dress you and lead you where you do not want to go." Jesus said this to indicate the kind of death by which Peter would glorify God. Then he said to him, "Follow me!"

THE SECOND CHANCE

WHEN PETE STOYANOVICH came on the field to try a long field goal, football fans all across the country were tuned in to the drama.

It was Thanksgiving Day, 1993. As traditional as turkey and dressing, the Dallas Cowboys were playing football that Thursday afternoon. Pete Stoyanovich was playing for the Cowboys' opponent that day, the Miami Dolphins. Both teams were having fabulous seasons, and the game was touted as a possible preview of that season's Super Bowl.

A freak snowstorm had added to the drama in Dallas. The game was sloppy because the field was frozen. The football itself was hard and slippery. But with time nearly running out, Miami had a chance to win the game. All they needed was for Stoyanovich to make the 41-yard field goal. Under normal conditions, it was almost a cinch. But with the bad weather, and the pressure of a big game, these were no normal conditions.

Dallas blocked the kick. Even then, it was a funny kind of block. The ball didn't career wildly backwards. Instead, it spun crazily to the side, and toward the Dallas goal line. It actually spun like a top for several seconds, a tantalizing target that no one was willing to touch. The Miami players couldn't touch it. They surrounded it, but they'd given up possession when Stoyanovich tried the field goal. The Dallas players stayed as far away from it as possible. As long as they didn't touch the ball, the game was practically over.

The only thing that would save Miami now . . . was big Leon Lett.

The Dallas defensive lineman lost his football senses, raced toward the ball, dropped to the turf and then slid like a 280-pound snowman toward the circle of Miami players.

When he got to the ball, his cold hands and the cold ball made for a chilling result. The ball bumped lazily toward the Dallas goal line and the Dolphin players fell on it. With just enough time to line up for another try, Stoyanovich kicked a short field goal to win the game, 16–14.

The obvious second-chance hero was the Miami kicker. Having missed one game-winning try, he made good on the second one.

Interesting thing about that season. Miami didn't win another game that year. Dallas won *all* of its remaining games, including that year's Super Bowl. One of the most important players on the team's championship run?

Leon Lett.

For a while, no one could find Lett after the Thanksgiving-Day blunder. "I was looking for Leon," said Dallas coach Jimmy Johnson. "Leon was back in the training room. This big 275-pound, 280-pounder had tears in his eyes. He was afraid he was going to get cut. So I grabbed him and said, 'Leon! You made a mistake, but hey—there were all kinds of mistakes in that game. You don't worry about it, because as long as I'm here, you're going to be a Dallas Cowboy.'"

Give a disappointed man like Pete Stoyanovich a second chance, you almost expect him to win the game. But give a humiliated man like Leon Lett a second chance, and don't be surprised if he doesn't take you to a championship trophy.

Meet the Leon Lett of the Bible. His name is Simon Peter.

Lett was one of the biggest players—literally—for his football team. Simon Peter was easily the biggest player for his team. Even if some of the other disciples could match his fisherman's bulk and strength, from a figurative point, there was no one bigger than Peter among the disciples.

Peter was always the leader of the group. He was the first to confess Jesus as the Messiah. He was the only disciple to walk on water. In fact, he was the only disciple to get out of the boat that night. He was the only disciple to pull out a weapon and attempt to use it when Jesus was arrested in the garden of Gethsemane.

Never mind that he tended to fumble every time he had a chance for glory. Just after Jesus congratulated Peter for having the courage to confess him as Messiah, Jesus embarrassed the big man by saying, "Get thee behind me, Satan!" Peter sank after only a few steps on the water, and in his brief fighting career, he only managed to remove an ear from a servant. Jesus repaired the ear while Peter ran for his life.

Still, he was the unquestioned leader of the disciples. During their last meal together, Peter had sworn that he would never leave Jesus. If necessary, he had declared, he would die for Jesus.

Jesus responded by predicting that before a rooster crowed twice, Peter would deny Jesus three times. And true to form, when the pressure was on, Peter slid like a clumsy lineman toward a ball he should have never touched. He denied Jesus once, twice, and then a third time. He got more intense with each denial. By the end, he "began to call down curses on himself and he swore to them, 'I don't know the man!'" (Matthew 26:73–75).

Luke's account adds that Jesus happened to step outside just as Peter's last words hung in the air, just as a rooster began to announce the coming day. "The Lord turned and looked straight at Peter. Then Peter . . . went outside and wept bitterly" (Luke 22:61–62).

The crucifixion followed, and Simon Peter was nowhere to be found. He didn't storm the Roman Praetorium and try to rescue Jesus. He didn't turn himself in and ask to die with his rabbi. He just hid himself away and lost his chance to be the hero he'd always vowed he would be, should the opportunity present itself.

When news of the resurrection began to sweep through Jerusalem Sunday morning, Peter was a very worried man. And after he encountered Jesus again?

He resigned.

That's what you're looking at when the curtain opens on John 21. Peter is fishing. He's led the way again, and several other disciples are with him. They're back where they were when Jesus had first called them, dropping their nets in the water, pulling up little more than driftwood, assuming that this will be their lot for the rest of their lives.

The very definition of a disciple in Jewish culture includes the detail that, if necessary, a disciple will die for his rabbi. He will do everything he can to look like his rabbi, act like his rabbi, and talk like his rabbi. Wherever the rabbi goes, the disciple goes. Why would a man ever try to walk on water?

Only because his rabbi is walking on the water. The idea of discipleship was so well understood, the real surprise about that day on the Sea of Galilee is not that Peter took a few steps on the water, but that all twelve disciples weren't stepping out of the boat.

A disciple gives up his life when he becomes a follower of a rabbi. Under no circumstances—*ever*—would he deny his relationship to his rabbi.

They had all denied. They had all run. They had all hidden. Only John was brave enough to spend time at the foot of the cross with the women who were there.

And so the disciples all returned to their trade, assuming that Jesus had no need of such bumbling, fumbling, cowardly disciples.

But Jesus came to them.

In the early morning hours, when it was still tough to make out the identity of anyone standing on the beach, Jesus prepared breakfast for the men who'd had a fruitless night of catching fish.

Three years earlier, Jesus had found them in the same situation.

He had asked them if they'd caught any fish, and offered that they might try the other side of the boat. It was Peter who had spoken up first—naturally—and it was Peter who had taken Jesus up on the challenge. When the nets became so full that they were breaking, he had fallen at Jesus' feet and asked for forgiveness. Jesus gave more than forgiveness. He offered Peter a chance to become his disciple.

"Follow me!" Jesus had said that day, and the next three years had been nothing short of amazing.

This time, after all the denials and mistakes and humiliation?

"Friends, haven't you any fish?"

No, they didn't have any fish. And no, they didn't really want any advice

from the shoreline . . . though something about the situation must have been unsettling. "Throw your net on the right side of the boat . . ." Jesus offered.

In a moment, fish were jumping into the net, and Peter was jumping out of the boat. He couldn't wait to get to Jesus.

They all ate breakfast, and then Jesus spent some extra time with his embarrassed disciple. Like a coach trying to comfort the goat of the game, he patiently worked with Peter.

His final challenge to Peter? It was exactly as the first. "Follow me!"

It was the ultimate second chance. Jesus might as well have said, "Hey, Peter, . . . would you like to try this again? Want to give it another shot? I'd like to keep you on the team. Think you're up to it?"

It wasn't an invitation only for Peter. It was for James and John, for Andrew and Thomas, for the rest of the disciples, and for every person who's ever tried to follow Jesus since that day.

Following Jesus isn't easy. It seems there's always a way to fumble. Always a way to mess up. Always the sound of roosters crowing, reminding us of how far short of God's glory we've fallen.

Peter and the other disciples were more than happy to take Jesus up on the offer of a second chance. As far as the Bible tells it, they never went fishing again. Instead, they changed the world.

Given a second chance, they endured prison time, scourgings, beatings, and even execution. They defied commands to stop telling the story of Jesus and they took the message to every corner of their world.

From cowards to champions, these men.

All because of a second chance.

Ever wanted a second chance with Jesus? He's the master of second chances, and perhaps no story better illustrates his incredible patience and mercy than the passage we've just studied in John 21.

When Peter and Jesus had a conversation on the beach, Jesus asked him three times, "Do you love me?" The three questions matched the three denials, and Peter was deeply hurt when they got to the third question. His shame was exposed, but only so his sin could be forgiven.

If you and Jesus were talking on the beach today, what sin might Jesus expose . . . in order that it might be forgiven? If you've immediately thought of a possibility, that's the one. Until there is a confession of sin, there can be no forgiveness of the sin. There can be no healing, no moving forward. Confess your sin to Jesus now, and be done with it.

How will you react to a Savior who loves you enough to keep asking you to, "Follow me," even if you feel as if you don't qualify as a worthy follower? Will you simply take advantage of the bottomless barrel of grace . . . or will you live as if this grace has made a difference in your life?

Live like a person who's just been given the best second chance you'll ever find.

Go change the world.

My God, my God, why have you forsaken me?
    Why are you so far from saving me,
    so far from the words of my groaning?
O my God, I cry out by day, but you do not answer,
    by night, and am not silent.
Yet you are enthroned as the Holy One;
    you are the praise of Israel.
In you our fathers put their trust;
    they trusted and you delivered them.
They cried to you and were saved;
    in you they trusted and were not disappointed.
But I am a worm and not a man,
    scorned by men and despised by the people.
All who see me mock me;
    they hurl insults, shaking their heads:
"He trusts in the LORD;
    let the LORD rescue him.
Let him deliver him,
    since he delights in him."

Yet you brought me out of the womb;

>you made me trust in you

>even at my mother's breast.

From birth I was cast upon you;

>from my mother's womb you have been my God.

Do not be far from me,

>for trouble is near

>and there is no one to help.

Many bulls surround me;

>strong bulls of Bashan encircle me.

Roaring lions tearing their prey

>open their mouths wide against me.

I am poured out like water,

>and all my bones are out of joint.

My heart has turned to wax;

>it has melted away within me.

My strength is dried up like a potsherd,

>and my tongue sticks to the roof of my mouth;

>you lay me in the dust of death.

Dogs have surrounded me;

>a band of evil men has encircled me,

>they have pierced my hands and my feet.

I can count all my bones;
> people stare and gloat over me.
They divide my garments among them
> and cast lots for my clothing.
But you, O LORD, be not far off;
> O my Strength, come quickly to help me.
Deliver my life from the sword,
> my precious life from the power of the dogs.
Rescue me from the mouth of the lions;
> save me from the horns of the wild oxen.
I will declare your name to my brothers;
> in the congregation I will praise you.
You who fear the LORD, praise him!
> All you descendants of Jacob, honor him!
> Revere him, all you descendants of Israel!
For he has not despised or disdained
> the suffering of the afflicted one;
he has not hidden his face from him
> but has listened to his cry for help.
From you comes the theme of my praise in the great assembly;
> before those who fear you will I fulfill my vows.

The poor will eat and be satisfied;
  they who seek the LORD will praise him—
  may your hearts live forever!
All the ends of the earth
  will remember and turn to the LORD,
and all the families of the nations
  will bow down before him,
for dominion belongs to the LORD
  and he rules over the nations.
All the rich of the earth will feast and worship;
  all who go down to the dust will kneel before him—
  those who cannot keep themselves alive.
Posterity will serve him;
  future generations will be told about the Lord.
They will proclaim his righteousness
  to a people yet unborn—
  for he has done it.

GOLGOTHA'S
RESIGNATIONS

T HERE ARE PRECIOUS FEW moments in a lifetime when it comes time to walk away.

Perhaps it's a long career that needs a retirement. It might be a mid-life change that calls for a resignation from one place, and a starting point in another. A pastor senses it's time to move to another ministry. A parent longs to be at home with the children. A student realizes another school would be the better choice for a course of study. A politician calls it a day and decides not to run for another term.

Whatever the case, there won't be many of these moments in an entire lifetime.

And when those moments come, they'll almost certainly come with a lot of emotion. Prayer and tears will mix with plans and excitement; an undercurrent of fear will fuel the adrenaline. People who see the change will take notice.

If you've been there, you know about the wild swing of emotions. You know about the careful thought, the slow process of change. You know how hard it is to actually make the decision, to take the drastic step. You also know that it takes tremendous motivation to cause such a change. To do so on the spur of the moment? The motivation would need to be traumatic.

There were at least two resignations at the cross. They were unexpected, sudden, and as dramatic as any change you've ever seen.

When Jesus died, two men decided it was time to walk away from the most prestigious jobs in Israel.

Perhaps you've heard of Nicodemus and Joseph.

Remember John 3:16, the most famous verse in the Bible? Jesus was describing God's love for the world through the gift of his son. The man who first heard those words? Nicodemus.

Joseph was the rich man who gave Jesus a decent burial. All four gospels tell of his generosity.

The Gospels also give us more details about who these men were.

The most important detail, by far, is this one. Both Nicodemus and Joseph were members of the ruling council, or the "Sanhedrin." Mark's gospel says Joseph was a "prominent member" of the council (Mark 15:43). John's introduction of Nicodemus includes the detail that Nicodemus, too, is a member of the council (John 3:1).

This may slip by us. So think "Congress." Think of a large body of very important men who make very important decisions. They are powerful, wealthy, and respected. In their world, to be a member of the Sanhedrin was about as good as it would ever get.

This was the same Sanhedrin that decided to do away with Jesus. This was the same group of rulers who had arranged for Jesus to be arrested, tried, and condemned. Jesus was an enemy of the state, and all who followed Jesus would be considered the same. When the disciples didn't stop telling the story of Jesus after his resurrection, it would be this same group that would have some of them arrested. In time, the Sanhedrin would arrange for the death of a deacon named Stephen, and even the execution of James, the brother of John and one of the original twelve disciples.

The idea that two members of this council would become followers of Jesus? It must have seemed preposterous. It was far too risky of a move. Men on the council had worked their entire lives to gain such a position. To be seen with Jesus, to defend him, was a good way to lose it all.

Perhaps that's why Nicodemus came to Jesus at night (John 3:2). Perhaps that's why Joseph was a secret disciple of Jesus (John 19:38).

But what happened at the cross that would cause both of these men to step out into the open, in front of eyewitnesses, and care for the body of Jesus as if they loved him?

Later, Joseph of Arimathea asked Pilate for the body of Jesus. Now Joseph was a disciple of Jesus, but secretly because he feared the Jews. With Pilate's permission, he came and took the body away. He was accompanied by Nicodemus, the man who earlier had visited Jesus at night. Nicodemus brought a mixture of myrrh and aloes, about seventy-five pounds. Taking Jesus' body, the two of them wrapped it, with the spices, in strips of linen. This was in accordance with Jewish burial customs. At the place where Jesus was crucified, there was a garden, and in the garden a new tomb, in which no one had ever been laid. Because it was the Jewish day of Preparation and since the tomb was nearby, they laid Jesus there. (John 19:38-42)

The Gospels tell us a lot of things about these two men, even though their part in the story was relatively brief.

We know Joseph was wealthy, and from a village named Arimathea. He also wasn't afraid to go to Pilate and ask permission for the body. Perhaps he was comfortable in circles of power and authority. We know he was in the process of carving out a new tomb for his family, and that the tomb wasn't yet completed. We know Nicodemus had already spoken up for Jesus in the council, at least to the point of wanting to give the man a fair hearing (John 7:50–51).

But there's another thing about Joseph and Nicodemus that's so obvious about them, the writers who speak of them don't even mention it.

Both men were students of the Text.

Like every other boy in their hometowns, they had been trained in the Torah. They had learned to revere it, obey it, and memorize it. Apparently, they graduated at the top of their class, for they were eventually elevated to positions on the Sanhedrin, the ruling board of all things religious. It's possible—and some would even say likely—that they had memorized thousands of verses of Scripture.

And it was the Text that caused both of these men to stop hiding, stop debating, and become very bold and visible followers of Jesus. It was the words of Scripture that caused them to resign from the Sanhedrin on the spot, if that would be the result of their actions that Friday afternoon.

Jesus could barely talk while he was on the cross. If you've done the research, you know that crucifixion victims have no position of comfort. As they hang on the cross, the pull on the arms and wrists is unbearable. In addition, there's no air for the lungs. But to push up for air means there will be unbearable pain on the feet. Since Jesus had been scourged, even the movement of shifting up and down on the wooden beam would have been unspeakably agonizing.

This is the genesis of the word *excruciating*. It literally means, "out of the cross." It's out of the experience Jesus knew, and he was living the nightmare for six long hours.

The gospel writers only record seven things Jesus said while he was on the cross. Perhaps he said more, but it's not hard to imagine that he didn't. How could a man in such excruciating pain clear his head enough to have a running conversation with those who were watching him die? A scream? Certainly. Intelligent conversation? Much more difficult.

And yet Jesus took time to ask for forgiveness for the very people who put him on the cross. He also asked John the disciple to take care of his mother.

And he had a short, but critically important conversation with one of the men who was dying beside him.

The other four things Jesus said? They were *all* quotations of Scripture.

"Into your hands I commit my spirit," Jesus said, quoting Psalm 31:5.

Nicodemus, Joseph, John, the mother of Jesus . . . they all knew the words. Anyone Jewish who was at the cross was hearing Jesus speak on two levels. He was speaking of his own situation *and* he was quoting Scripture.

The Roman soldiers would have missed it. We miss it. Such a love for Scripture was not the Romans' way of life, and it is not our way of life. The absolute reverence and knowledge serious students of the Text had in those days is almost indescribable.

So when Jesus cried out, "My God, my God, why have you forsaken me?" The Jewish listeners *did not* hear a theological statement about God somehow turning his back on Jesus during that darkest hour. What they heard was the opening line of Psalm 22. As students who had memorized the entire psalm, they instantly reflected on other phrases in the song. They connected with what Jesus was doing. He was telling them to check the Text. He was asking that they look again at the ancient words, to see that his death was no accident.

It wasn't the only time on the cross that Jesus did such a thing. Though he had said, "I thirst," he had turned his face away from the soaked sponge that offered him relief. Was he really pointing the people who knew the Text back to Psalm 22? After all, it described a man whose "strength is dried up like a potsherd," whose "tongue sticks to the roof of my mouth." And when Jesus announced, "It is finished," he was also echoing the final words of Psalm 22 . . . "He has done it."

Think like a Jewish person who'd grown up with the Scripture. It would have been instinctive. They would have gone over all the words of the familiar phrases. They would have heard Jesus saying, in a sense, "Check the Text! Look at the Text!"

So check the Text. Read of a crowd scorning a condemned man, shaking their heads and mocking him. Read of one who had been brought out of the womb by God, cast upon God from the first moment of life. Connect with words that describe a man with all his bones out of joint, one who was "poured out like water." Slow down as you come to the image of one whose hands and feet have been pierced. Comprehend the reality that a psalm written a thousand years before described a man watching his tormentors divide his garments among them, even casting lots for his clothing.

It all happened to Jesus, while he was on the cross, and he quoted the psalm that had foretold every detail.

And yet there was hope, for Psalm 22 also promised that "future generations will be told about the Lord." Even as you read these words, we are seeing fulfillment of the promise!

There is more, but even this sampling is stunning. Add to the mix that David penned the words four hundred years before anyone on the planet had ever been crucified. How did he write such words except by the leading of God's Spirit?

Jesus was a rabbi to the last moment, still teaching his

listeners about the Text. When he quoted the first line of Psalm 22, it was no accident, and it was no cry of ultimate loneliness.

Jesus was pointing all who would hear him back to the words so often called "the Word of God." He pointed them back to a place that seemed to say, "This was the plan. It might look out of control, but it's not. It's exactly what had to happen, and to make sure you get this, Psalm 22 was recorded on the pages you memorized as children."

It's easy to see Nicodemus and Joseph looking at one another as they heard Jesus' words. Their minds raced to the Text. Maybe they thought of other related Scriptures. Did Joseph remember that Isaiah had even promised that the Messiah would one day be laid in a rich man's tomb?

> *He was assigned a grave with the wicked,*
>   *and with the rich in his death. (Isaiah 53:9)*

Whether he remembered Isaiah's promise or not, there had been enough of a message communicated—through Scripture—at the cross to cause both men to resign everything. If they lost their positions of high influence, so be it. If Joseph's wealth would take a blow because of his actions, so be it. If they would suffer along with the disciples, they would accept their fate.

Because there at Golgotha, they discovered something much more important than either one of them already had, or ever would have.

They found the promised Messiah.

When you find him, resignation is the only proper response. When you really discover him, quitting everything else is exactly what happens.

Your goals are shelved. His instructions are followed. Your priorities are canceled. His priorities are more important. Money? It belongs to him. Same for your family. Same for your very life.

Perhaps walking away from the Sanhedrin hadn't been part of the plan for Joseph and Nicodemus that Friday morning. But by Friday evening, they had made a decision. They would rather carry a corpse of the Savior they loved than to sit inside one more meeting with the spiritual corpses they once had tried so hard to impress.

Golgotha. The place of the skull. The place of the crucifixion.

The place where resignations happen, and everything changes.

MAKE THE LESSON YOUR OWN

When Jesus cried out, "My God, my God, why have you forsaken me?" he was obviously quoting the first words of Psalm 22.

But was God the Father turning his back on Jesus, the Son? If Jesus really did want us to look at the Text and read Psalm 22, perhaps we'd better read it all again, over and over, until we see every nuance.

Included in this psalm is a declaration of faith:

> *You who fear the LORD, praise him!*
>   *All you descendants of Jacob, honor him!*
>   *Revere him, all you descendants of Israel!*
> *For he has not despised or disdained*
>   *the suffering of the afflicted one;*
> *he has not hidden his face from him*
>   *but has listened to his cry for help.*
>   *(Psalm 22:23–24, emphasis added)*

And sure enough, by Sunday evening, Jesus was standing before his disciples, resurrected and alive. He had not been despised, disdained, or forgotten.

He had been on a mission.

Standing at the foot of the cross, and remembering the words of Psalm 22, Nicodemus and Joseph finally understood the mission. Perhaps they remembered more passages that described the Messiah's place of birth, his actions, his miracles, and his death. Maybe they finally understood Isaiah 53 in light of Jesus' death.

Faced with that kind of revelation, they were more than ready to leave a group of men who ruled Israel, but who had missed the Messiah.

Is there anything in your life that is more important than following Jesus? Is there anything you cherish— perhaps a job, a reputation, a relationship, or even your money—that has a higher priority to you than following the Messiah?

If so, a resignation is called for.

Either follow him the way he deserves to be followed, or quit calling yourself a follower.

— MATTHEW 4:18–22 —

As Jesus was walking beside the Sea of Galilee, he saw two brothers, Simon called Peter and his brother Andrew. They were casting a net into the lake, for they were fishermen. "Come, follow me," Jesus said, "and I will make you fishers of men." At once they left their nets and followed him.

Going on from there, he saw two other brothers, James son of Zebedee and his brother John. They were in a boat with their father Zebedee, preparing their nets. Jesus called them, and immediately they left the boat and their father and followed him.

ALL IN

A FEW YEARS BACK, a new football coach came to Auburn University. His name was Gene Chizik, and he arrived in Alabama's heartland with a passionate desire to turn the university's struggling football program around.

It didn't take him long. Just two seasons later, Auburn raced to an undefeated season and the national championship.

No doubt, it helped that Auburn had an incredible lineup of talented football players. But at the heart of the team's turnaround was Chizik's challenge to his team, to the university, and to all of its fans to be "all in."

It doesn't take a university degree to figure out what he meant. Immediately, players, fans, and the entire support community of the school bought into the idea that they would be "all in." For players, it would be a 100 percent effort on every play. They would practice the same way. They would train in the off-season as if each day was critically important to the team's success.

Professors, administrators, and students were challenged to get behind the team like they'd never been before. The band caught the spirit, and every note was just a bit crisper that season. Every drummer was right on the mark. The cheerleaders jumped higher. The hot dogs were hotter, the weather was better, the restrooms cleaner.

Everyone at Auburn, for one magical season, was "all in." So maybe it shouldn't surprise us that a national championship was in order, or that the team's star quarterback won the Heisman Trophy. When everyone's on board with all they've got, outstanding success is practically the only option for how things will eventually turn out.

Picture Jesus as the coach, and the young men he called as disciples as his players. The image might be more accurate than you'd first think. Most of the disciples were very young. We know of only one who was married. Peter, you'll remember, had a mother-in-law. Jesus healed her when he arrived in Capernaum (Matthew 8:14–15). Perhaps other disciples were married, but the text doesn't indicate that, and the tradition of the day was for disciples of a rabbi to be young men, perhaps of today's high-school age.

The point is, when Jesus invited Peter, James, John, Andrew, and the rest to follow him, it was an "all-in" proposal. "Follow me," he would say, and then he'd start walking. Those hearing the invitation could either stay where they were, or follow. There was no other option.

Some would choose not to follow. The Bible's record indicates that a lot of people couldn't make the "all-in" commitment. One young man had just gotten married. Another wanted to bury his father. One had a lot of money, and when Jesus challenged him to give it all away, the young man couldn't do it. One man Jesus healed wanted nothing more than to follow Jesus, but Jesus wanted him to stay in his community and tell others what had happened.

Sounds pretty tough, doesn't it?

It *was* tough. It's still tough.

"All-in" with Jesus may have meant that Peter left his young wife, at least for the seasons when he was away from Capernaum. On the other hand, she might have traveled with Jesus and the disciples, at least some of the time. Women definitely were a part of the traveling group (see Luke 8:2–3), so maybe Peter's wife came along, too. Even if she never traveled with Jesus, she let Peter go with him. No doubt, she was "all-in," too.

"All-in" meant Andrew, Peter, James, and John left the family business. Who was left behind to provide a living for their family? Whoever it was, if they supported the decision of a family member to follow Jesus, they were "all-in," too.

So here's what a disciple does. Once he or she makes the decision to follow a rabbi, then every action, from that point on, is affected by the rabbi. The goal would be to act like the rabbi, talk like the rabbi, respond to every crisis like the rabbi, and even to walk like the rabbi.

If your rabbi limps, you limp. If he gets up and begins walking, follow him. If he asks you to do something, you'll do it. It wouldn't be surprising to find disciples following their rabbi to the men's room. After all, this is a part of life, too, and how the rabbi spends his time in the men's room is how a disciple would want to spend some time in a men's room!

Sound ridiculous? A Talmudic anecdote actually tells of a disciple who hid

under his master's bed. According to the satirical story, the young man wanted to learn how to properly make love by watching the rabbi and his wife! The rabbi threw the disciple out, but the point is made. If you're all-in as a disciple, then nothing in life is off-limits. *Everything* will be affected by your decision to follow.

There's a question that troubles me. What if the definition of a genuine disciple is "all-in"? What if the criteria for who gets into heaven is based on the all-in standard? Would the majority of people in our churches—or even in our pulpits—qualify?

There came a last night for Jesus and the disciples. It came upon them suddenly, with shocking speed. They gathered around a Passover meal and remembered the exodus of God's people. All over Jerusalem that night, thousands of families were doing the same thing. They would eat the world's most symbolic meal, and in the process, consume four cups of wine. Each cup came at a particular point in the process. Each one was a marker along the way of remembering God's great work of salvation, when his people were held in bondage by the Egyptians.

Jesus set one of those four cups aside and, after the meal, held it up as a final symbol that he, too, was "all-in."

"This is my blood," he said.

There is nothing more a man can give, once he gives his blood. If he gives it all, his life is finished. Indeed, by the next night, Jesus had bled out on the cross. It had been a horrible day of blood-letting. He had been beaten, scourged, and crucified. Even after his death, a soldier pierced his side with his spear, and blood that had already separated because of the death process poured out.

It took a while for the lesson to soak in. Only after the resurrection did the disciples put the symbolism together. God's people might have been set free from Egyptian bondage, but slavery to sin had been an even more difficult way of life. And sin could hold a person captive all the way through eternity! This time, Jesus would be the way of salvation. This time, Jesus would be the ultimate sacrifice, the very embodiment of God's saving grace. He was, as Paul would later write, the ultimate Passover Lamb (1 Corinthians 5:7).

The cup holds a question, every time we hold it. Whether you're celebrating Passover as a follower of Jesus, or remembering "the Lord's Supper" with other followers in a typical Christian church, the cup demands an answer.

Are you "all-in" . . . or not?

If you're going to follow your rabbi, you will do your dead-level best to look like him, act like him, talk like him, respond like him, give like him, love like him . . . there will be no part of life that is exempt from modeling your rabbi. You will never leave him, forsake him, or deny him. As a matter of fact, if necessary, you will die for him.

For that's what it means to be "all-in."

The next time you partake of Communion, pay particular attention to the elements. And listen to the question the cup continues to ask. Are you all-in . . . or not? This is a new way of phrasing the Bible's insistence that we not take the elements of the Lord's Supper casually. As Paul put it, "Whoever eats the bread or drinks the cup of the Lord in an unworthy manner will be guilty of sinning against the body and blood of the Lord. A man ought to examine himself before he eats of the bread and drinks of the cup" (1 Corinthians 11:27–28).

On the other hand, if we waited until we were perfectly and completely committed to following Jesus with everything we've got, none of us would probably ever take the cup again. Another part of this lesson is caught up in how the disciples acted within a few hours after taking that cup that symbolized the blood of Jesus. As you almost certainly know, they all ran away! When Jesus needed them the most, there was barely a scuffle. They ran for their lives, and hid in the shadows for the rest of the weekend.

Could it be that this is why so many of them had returned to their fishing nets after the resurrection (John 21)? The last chapter of John's gospel tells us that Simon Peter, Thomas, Nathanael, James, John, and two other disciples were fishing on the Sea of Galilee. They had all been overjoyed by the resurrection, of course. But wouldn't they have all felt disqualified from following Jesus again? They had violated every tenet of what it means to follow a rabbi. Though he had promised to die with Jesus, if necessary, Simon Peter had denied him vehemently. Thomas didn't believe until his own eyes had seen the hard evidence. The others had also all fallen far short of what it means to be a disciple.

Me, too.

There's a chance, right here, to believe that you and I might never make the grade. That we might never be "good enough." The disciples certainly felt that way from time to time, and never more so than after their group denials at the cross. After the resurrection, after the joy subsided, they all assumed they were off the team. Many of them even started fishing again, the job they'd had before Jesus asked them to follow him.

But if you know the story, you know Jesus didn't give up on them. In fact, Jesus gave them the job of telling the world about his message, and then Jesus left. The entire message of good news was in the hands of people who thought they were disqualified from following.

This is grace.

Bolstered by forgiveness, they never failed so miserably again. In fact, they succeeded far beyond their wildest dreams! They changed the world.

Grace motivated them. God's Spirit empowered them. And in time, they looked amazingly like their rabbi.

This *is* possible.

So follow your rabbi.

Go "all-in."

— MATTHEW 16:13–20 —

When Jesus came to the region of Caesarea Philippi, he asked his disciples, "Who do people say the Son of Man is?"

They replied, "Some say John the Baptist; others say Elijah; and still others, Jeremiah or one of the prophets."

"But what about you?" he asked. "Who do you say I am?"

Simon Peter answered, "You are the Christ, the Son of the living God."

Jesus replied, "Blessed are you, Simon son of Jonah, for this was not revealed to you by man, but by my Father in heaven. And I tell you that you are Peter, and on this rock I will build my church, and the gates of Hades will not overcome it. I will give you the keys of the kingdom of heaven; whatever you bind on earth will be bound in heaven, and whatever you loose on earth will be loosed in heaven." Then he warned his disciples not to tell anyone that he was the Christ.

STORMING THE
GATES OF HADES

IT'S SAFE TO SAY none of the disciples had ever been to Caesarea Philippi. John was too young. If his mother had known Jesus had planned to go there she seriously might have put a stop to the field trip. And Peter? Think his wife would have approved of a trip to a place that had the worst reputation in Israel?

When Matthew wrote about the day, he announced it with little fanfare. "When Jesus came to the region of Caesarea Philippi . . ." (Matthew 16:13).

And that's it.

No mention of the sordid reputation of pagan practices from centuries past. No description of the Greek gods displayed along the waterfront, or of the brand-new temple to Caesar Augustus, one of the first in the world to ever honor a Roman emperor as god. Even today, two thousand years later, the niches cut into the cliff are still visible, still a clear reminder of how many gods once called Caesarea Philippi home.

And it's interesting that Matthew avoided the traditional name of the place. They called it "Banias," or even "Panias," in recognition of the days when the priests of the demonic Pan danced across the flat stones around the cliffs. How wild was the worship of Pan, the god believed to be half man and half goat? It should provide a hint that the word "panic" can be traced back this cult. This was a god of fear, and his terror still echoed across the northern hills of Israel.

There's not a photo of the place in the Bible, either, so unless you knew that this was where the Jordan River began, you'd miss that critically important piece of the puzzle. And what of nearby Dan? It was home to one of the two golden calves that started the downfall of the Northern Kingdom.

Caesarea Philippi? Physically, it was as far away from Jerusalem and the temple as you could get and still be in Israel. Spiritually, it was even further away.

So why would Jesus take his disciples there?

It was rabbinical teaching at its best. Jesus walked his team forty-five miles on an uphill path just to ask them two questions. As it turns out, the environment of the questions adds amazing depth to the story.

Surrounded by Greek gods, Roman gods, with the echoes of the worst pagan religions Israel had ever known still reverberating, Jesus wanted to know, "Who do people say that I am?"

The disciples had heard the opinions around Capernaum, and they offered them up.

"Some say you're a prophet."

"I heard someone call you Elijah."

"I've heard you compared to Jeremiah."

"Rumor has it that you're John the Baptizer come back to life."

Jesus cut the answers off. "But what about you?" he asked. "Who do you say that I am?"

And this was the reason they'd come so far. In a cafeteria of religion, which course was Jesus? In the thousand-piece puzzle of all things spiritual, which piece would the teacher from the Galilee be? In a world not protected by godly parents and faithful synagogue leaders, far away from the safe confines of home, what would they say about Jesus now?

Simon was the first one to cross the line. "You're the Christ. You're the one we've waited for." Surrounded by stone gods that couldn't even speak, Peter declared that Jesus was the Son of the living God.

This is the heart of Matthew's gospel.

This is the moment Simon becomes the leader of the Jesus movement and the leader of his peers. For his willingness to say what they were all thinking, Jesus even gave him a new name. We have known this man as Simon Peter all these centuries because Jesus gave him the second name at Caesarea Philippi.

"Peter" was "Cephas" in their language, and "Rock" in every language. It was nearly a nickname, this "Rocky" moniker.

There was a huge play on words going on, and unless you ever get the opportunity to stand on the rocks of Caesarea Philippi, you might miss it.

In a land of rocks, Caesarea is a massive rock. On the floor, around the first few paces of the Jordan River, the rock is flat and smooth. The dramatic cliff that frames the beginning of the river is rock from top to bottom. And the setting is in the shadows of Mt. Hermon, the largest mountain in the land.

So in a rock-solid setting, Jesus called Peter "the Rock."

It stuck, and Simon Peter has been revered ever since that day. Jesus gave Peter the "keys to the kingdom" that day, and a short speech on the importance of forgiveness. From that scene came the belief that Jesus set aside Peter as the first Pope for Catholics. On the other side of a very long church argument, Protestants came to see Peter's confession as the foundation for the church.

As is often the case, the church missed the main point altogether.

The truth is, Peter was the leader of the disciples. He led courageously and effectively after the resurrection, and according to church tradition, died as a martyr. And the truth is, his confession of faith is critically important. Jesus once said, "If you confess me before men, I'll confess you before my father in heaven. But if you will not confess me before men, I will not confess you before my Father in heaven" (see Matthew 10:32–33). Standing at judgment, you won't find anything more important than a confession of Jesus as Lord.

And yet there is something hidden here in plain sight.

It's all the rock. Caesarea Philippi is one giant, impossible-to-hide rock. The rocks had been carved into columns and pedestals for all the wrong gods. The cliff had been fashioned for temples and niches for pagan gods. It's possible they were standing there, looking at the massive buildings, watching the worship of pretend gods, when Jesus said, "On this rock, I'll build my church."

Think of Jesus saying something like this. "Guys, they never thought we'd come up here. Matter of fact, *you* never thought we'd come here. Your families had no idea this trip was part of the plan. This place is so pagan, packed with so much evil history, it's the one place you never, ever thought you'd see. But we came. And we're here. We're not going away, either. We're going to build the church right here."

You want a spiritual war? Jesus fired the first shot.

"And the Gates of Hades will not overcome us."

As it turns out, it's another secret hidden in plain view. The most prominent feature at Caesarea Philippi is a huge, dark cave. For centuries, the river rushed from the depths of the cave. But on the first day of 1837, a devastating earthquake in Tiberias shook all the way to Banias, closing off the underground river and forcing the water to make a much wider entrance to the open air. While the picture is still impressive, we can't see what Jesus and the disciples would have seen.

But try to imagine it.

It was a dark cave. It appeared to be bottomless, and it flowed with an eternal supply of water, which was life to the nation. It was, in a sense, a source of eternal life.

In a twist of demonic irony, this life-giving cave had become home to a long list of pagan gods. Besides Pan, Baal and Asherah were a part of the picture, too. If you've read the Hebrew Text, you've seen their names many times. The worship of all these gods? It was incredibly evil. According to one of the psalms, "They sacrificed their sons and their daughters to demons" (Psalm 106:37).

It's hard to imagine the evil that must have been a part of the history of

Caesarea Philippi. From the sexual deviancy to the sacrifice of infants, this place had become one of the darkest places the world had ever known. In one way, it was the center of the darkness.

For the great cave of Caesarea Philippi had become known as the entrance to the underworld. To Hades. This, they said, was the gateway to hell. It was the "Gate of Hades."

Listen again to what Jesus said.

> *"On this rock I will build my church, and the gates of Hades will not overcome it."* (Matthew 16:18)

No doubt, it was the first trip the disciples had made to the Gateway of the underworld. No doubt, it was their first look at pagan temples built to honor stone gods and emperors as if they had created life.

But did you understand what Jesus was telling his men? It would not be their last trip! They would bring the fight to the enemy, and any "gate" built to keep them out would be defenseless against the attack.

It was heady stuff, and the lesson stuck. In time, that small group of disciples led a growing movement of Jesus followers, and a kingdom of righteousness took root. Caesarea Philippi died with the passage of empires, cults, and earthquakes.

But the message of Jesus is still here. It is still changing lives, often in the darkest places of any community.

The Gates of Hades at Caesarea Philippi have literally crumbled. All that is left of a once pagan society are the broken rocks and ruins that remind us of all the evil that once happened there.

But the church? It lives. The movement Jesus started is stronger than ever, and the world is a different place because of the impact billions of believers have made in the years that followed two key questions once asked in the shadow of the "Gates of Hades."

The invitation to be a part of the spiritual battle against the darkness represented there has been passed on to us.

All too often, the "church" actually gets in the way of accomplishing the mission Jesus set in front of us.

Jesus didn't ask for a building to be built at Caesarea Philippi. He asked for the "church" to go to places where the message of hope and grace most needed to be communicated, and to make a difference there.

Is there a place in your community that seems reprehensible to you? If so, is there a way to "storm the gates" through ministry, love, and compassion? Is there something you could do other than pray that the business would go away? Some of the world's most effective ministries have come when God's people moved away from complaining about a problem in their community and into a way of addressing the problem by ministering to the people most affected by the issue at hand.

If Jesus were leading disciples today, would he hold protest signs outside a strip club, or organize a ministry to those who feel trapped by the lifestyle? If he took your community of faith to a modern-day "Gates of Hades," where would that be, and what would he ask you to do?

Is there any reason you can't get started with the ministry that comes to mind? Be sure you're covered in prayer, and that you seek the guidance of other believers. But if God leads you to move forward with a new ministry, be assured of one thing, right now.

The gates of Hades don't stand a chance.

ACTS 24:27

When two years had passed, Felix was succeeded by Porcius Festus, but because Felix wanted to grant a favor to the Jews, he left Paul in prison.

ROMANS 8:28

And we know that in all things God works for the good of those who love him, who have been called according to his purpose.

ALL THINGS
FOR GOOD

EVEN NOW, the rich and famous come to Caesarea.

Where Herod the Great once built a stunning palace for himself, Caesarea is still home to some of the most expensive real estate in Israel. Modern-day "palaces" dot the landscape.

Where kings once watched gladiators battle for sport in Caesarea's stadiums, today's residents watch golfers do battle at the most exclusive club in the land.

And as hard as it is to imagine, in the very same theater where crowds heard concerts two thousand years ago, the arts live again. The three-thousand-seat theater was unearthed in the 1960s, refurbished, and today hosts a wide variety of musicians, all performing in front of the breathtaking backdrop of the Mediterranean Sea.

In a sense, the ancient ruins have come back to life, and those ruins leave no doubt about the nature of Herod's Caesarea. It was the playground of kings, the envy of the Middle East, and a home away from home for Roman royalty. Built nearly from scratch, the city was home to the latest technology and architecture of its day. The man-made port was a gateway to international travelers, and Caesarea quickly became the largest and most important city in Israel.

If you're looking for beauty, look no further. With the sparkling waters of the Mediterranean as its backdrop, Caesarea must have been one of the most beautiful cities in the entire world.

Unless, of course, Caesarea is your prison.

Luke's record of the first generation of Christians tells us Paul was taken to Caesarea after a riot in Jerusalem, and held there for two years. His case was heard before multiple parties before Paul finally grew so frustrated with the system that he appealed his case to the highest court in his world.

As a Roman citizen, he elected to use his right to appeal to the caesar himself.

The appeal was Paul's ticket out of Caesarea, and apparently the first sentence of the last chapter of his life. According to the Bible, two more years of house arrest followed in Rome. According to church tradition, once Paul made it to the emperor's court, he lost his life at the emperor's hand. Whether that happened immediately or a few years later is unknown.

But what is known is this. The most successful church planter in Christian history spent the last years of his life in confinement.

Instead of starting even more churches, Paul waited for yet another person in authority to review his case. Instead of checking on his network of young churches and young pastors, Paul was stuck in Caesarea. He was just a short walk away from the ships that could have taken him on another journey for God, but God allowed him to go nowhere at all. He was in one of the most beautiful places in the world, but he couldn't enjoy any of the beauty.

On the surface, it was a season of life that simply didn't need to happen.

How many times did Paul ask the most obvious, most repeated question of life?

Why?

Why would a good God allow such a frustrating season to his best worker?

Why would a wise God stop the most successful spread of the gospel the world has ever seen so Paul could spend his days counting the days?

Maybe you've asked some similar questions.

Instead of chains in a Roman cell, it was a hospital bed that kept you pinned down.

Instead of a bustling city by the ocean, it was a small village in the country, far away from your dreams of big-city success.

Maybe it was circumstances that stopped you cold. Just when things could have gone so right, they went horribly wrong.

Would you relate to Paul, the Christian rock star of the book of Acts, the man stopped dead in his tracks at the very peak of his career?

Perhaps it would be intriguing to take something Paul wrote his friends in Italy and read it back to him, while time wasted away in Caesarea.

"And we know that in all things," Paul wrote in Romans 8:28, "God works for the good of those who love him, who have been called according to his purpose."

"So Paul," we'd love to ask, looking at the little man through the prison bars, "how is God working good *now*?"

I doubt Paul could have answered your question then any more than you might be able to answer your questions now. I would suspect that Paul would be as frustrated—even as angry—as you might be one day with your set of tough breaks.

And yet he wrote the words, and we have clung to them for hope ever since we heard them.

Of course, we actually have an advantage over Paul at this point. We can see what has happened over the past two thousand years, and how God used even the prison years of Paul's life for good.

The letters Paul wrote to his brand-new churches, explaining what it was to be a church? Many of them became part of the Christian text. In fact, Paul wrote thirteen of the New Testament's twenty-seven "books."

When did he have time to write? In prison, of course. Even more importantly, when did he have time to think through all the complex issues of God's amazing work of salvation? Could it be that Paul would never have written such valuable insight unless difficult circumstances had literally made him sit still for a few years?

Could Paul have known then that his letters would have far more impact than he ever intended? Here we are, two thousand years later, still memorizing some of the most important words the Christian community has ever received.

Most of those words were written when Paul was "wasting time" in Caesarea.

And what of Paul's friend Luke?

According to Luke's own record in the book of Acts, he apparently met Paul in Greece and traveled with him for the rest of Paul's life. By this timeline, Paul wasn't the only one with time on his hands while he was under guard in Caesarea.

Luke was just as delayed as Paul while the authorities took their time deciding what to do with their prisoner.

Luke should be a familiar name to you. He wrote the "gospel of Luke," which is the longest (by a count of words) of the four historical accounts of the life of Jesus. And yet Luke wasn't an eyewitness to any of those stories. He never met Jesus. He also wrote "Acts," which is the story of what happened after Jesus left his followers to carry out his mission.

So how did he gather up all that information?

Could two years be enough time to meet some of the disciples, read some of the other manuscripts, visit the Sea of Galilee, interview some aging shepherds in Bethlehem, and organize the stories into his massive account of the life of Jesus and the first years of the early church?

It's possible, and maybe even *probable*.

Bottom line, Luke found time somewhere to gather a massive amount of information, organize it, write it, and preserve the history of both the life of Jesus and the first generation of activity by the early church.

If not for Luke, we would be missing an enormous amount of information. We would not know about the parable of the prodigal, we wouldn't know about angels singing to shepherds outside of Bethlehem, and we wouldn't know about the Day of Pentecost. For that matter, we might even wonder who this "Paul" was that kept writing so many letters.

When you look back on Paul's time in Caesarea that way, it's actually a good thing that he spent two years in prison there. It's quite conceivable that Paul would look back on the time now and see the impact his letters from prison have had over the past twenty centuries. It's entirely plausible that he would see Luke's time of investigating the stories and think of his delay in Caesarea as a very good thing.

Or maybe he did see it. Maybe he and Luke talked about the good things that were coming out of what appeared to be bad circumstances.

After all, he and Silas had already made it a habit to sing during their prison experiences (Acts 16 has that story). And he had spent a lot of time working through all the things he'd come to know as life-changing truth.

Among the lessons? One you'd be wise to grasp, no matter what difficult circumstances you might be facing today.

"And we know that in all things, God works for the good of those who love him, who have been called according to his purpose."

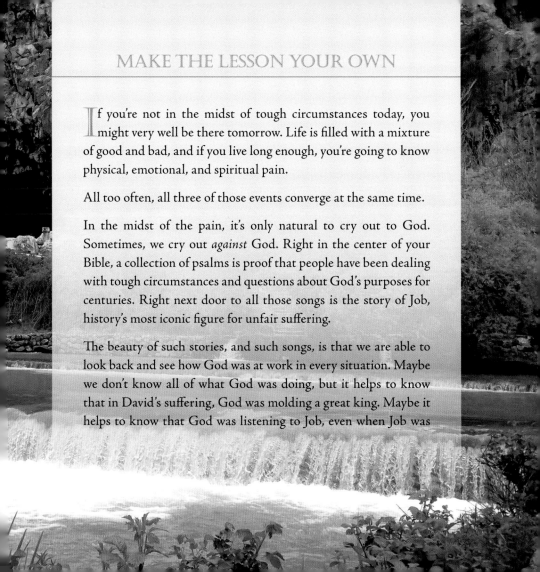

MAKE THE LESSON YOUR OWN

If you're not in the midst of tough circumstances today, you might very well be there tomorrow. Life is filled with a mixture of good and bad, and if you live long enough, you're going to know physical, emotional, and spiritual pain.

All too often, all three of those events converge at the same time.

In the midst of the pain, it's only natural to cry out to God. Sometimes, we cry out *against* God. Right in the center of your Bible, a collection of psalms is proof that people have been dealing with tough circumstances and questions about God's purposes for centuries. Right next door to all those songs is the story of Job, history's most iconic figure for unfair suffering.

The beauty of such stories, and such songs, is that we are able to look back and see how God was at work in every situation. Maybe we don't know all of what God was doing, but it helps to know that in David's suffering, God was molding a great king. Maybe it helps to know that God was listening to Job, even when Job was convinced God was deaf. And maybe it helps to see how powerfully God was working even when Paul thought all work had come to a screeching halt in Caesarea.

Maybe.

Tough circumstances are so very difficult, you might not see any good coming out of them.

This is where faith comes into play. This is where we hold on to Bible verses like Romans 8:28 and believe that God is in control, even when there is no apparent evidence of it.

In time, we might see the good coming out of the bad. In time, we might reflect on the amazing way God works in all circumstances.

But in the midst of the struggle, there is an opportunity for faith.

Here's your assignment. Start noticing all the times when bad things happened to the very good people in the Bible. You'll find that none of them were exempt. All of them suffered in some way, and some of them even died as a result of their love for God. As you read their stories, watch the reaction. Watch the process of the struggle, and for most of them, the choice of faith.

They endured prison time and physical mistreatment, considering it a privilege to suffer for their faith in Jesus. They took on impossible tasks, changed everything about their lives, and entered into the most joyful season of life they had ever known. They lost land, they were forced to move, and they lost the people they loved the most. Still, they clung to their belief that God was in control, even when they couldn't see the entire plan.

They changed the world, and lived amazingly victorious lives.

Simply by choosing faith.

This is our choice, too. It is our turn to be a generation of faithful followers who believe that in all things, God is still able to work for good for those who love him and are called according to his purposes.

Choose faith.

ABOUT THE
AUTHOR

ANDY COOK has a passion for the land of the Bible. The pastor from Georgia leads hiking tours in Israel as often as possible, and his video lessons recorded there have been broadcast across the country on the Christian Television Network. He is the founder of Experience Israel Now, Inc., a ministry that seeks to "bring Israel" to those who can't make the trip.

Middle Georgia knows Cook as the pastor of Shirley Hills Baptist Church, and its biggest ambassador for Israel. When the area held its first-ever gathering of synagogues and churches to celebrate the birthday of modern-day Israel, Cook was the keynote speaker. For years, his church also welcomed ten thousand people each Christmas to a life-sized re-creation of Bethlehem.

The author of three other books, Cook is also a regular contributor of sermons for LifeWay.com. Before he became a pastor, he edited the first series of sports articles to ever win a Pulitzer Prize while he was sports editor of *The Macon Telegraph*.

But if you ask him about the important things, he'll tell you about his family. He and Melody have three daughters, one son-in-law, and grandchildren who've stolen their hearts. On the best of days, you'll likely find him spending time on his tractor, listening to Chris Tomlin on his iPod, and planning yet another trip to Jerusalem.

Discover more at experienceisraelnow.com or pastorandycook.com.

PHOTO INDEX